Super Mario Bros. 2

Super Mario Bros. 2

Jon Irwin

Boss Fight Books
Los Angeles, CA
bossfightbooks.com

ISBN 13: 978-1-940535-05-0
First Printing: 2014
Second Printing: 2016

Series Editor: Gabe Durham
Book Design by Ken Baumann
Page Design by Adam Robinson

For Elizabeth,
who taught me the difference

PLEASE SELECT

FOREWORD

Video games have played a huge role in my life. As Nintendo's Gamemaster, I played and analyzed every game developed by and for Nintendo prior to 1991. During that period, I developed a deep understanding of games and the rich personal experiences they provided players. I knew key staff well at Nintendo of America and, to a limited degree, Nintendo Co., Ltd. in Kyoto, Japan. I considered then-president of Nintendo of America Minoru Arakawa (Mr. A) to be my friend. The story and history Jon Irwin recounts in this book I lived firsthand.

I first met Mario as Jumpman in the arcade hit *Donkey Kong* while serving as warehouse and shipping manager for Nintendo of America in 1981. The *Donkey Kong* arcade game quickly became a phenomenal hit in the US. Initially manufactured in Japan and shipped through the Nintendo of America warehouse in Seattle, Washington, *Donkey Kong* was so successful that for a brief period Nintendo was the largest-volume shipper through the Port of Seattle.

By the time Shigeru Miyamoto's *Super Mario Bros.* was released in 1985, my role as shipping and warehouse manager had expanded to include reviewing with a Western eye all new Japanese Nintendo products, arcade games, Game & Watch handheld games, and Famicom games, reporting my results to Mr. A.

In the early spring of 1985, Mr. A gave me a box of 40-some-odd Nintendo Famicom games and asked me to play each one and recommend which games should become launch titles for the Nintendo Entertainment System in the US. The story of the launch of the NES is longer than this foreword allows, but of the games in that box, it was *Super Mario Bros.* that made the biggest impression.

My experience with *Super Mario Bros. 2* began in the summer of 1986 when I received a new box from Nintendo that contained yet another set of new titles for both the Famicom and the recently released Famicom Disc System. One of these Famicom discs was *Super Mario Bros. 2.*

I was surprised that the disc had arrived at my desk without any fanfare or advance warning. After all, it was the sequel to the NES's most popular game. I quickly loaded the game and began playing. What came next was completely unexpected.

I was immediately killed by a mushroom that, unlike the mushrooms in *Super Mario Bros.*, was now poisonous. Chagrinned but undaunted, I continued playing only to be taken by a strong, unpredictable wind and tossed into a chasm. Soon after, I succumbed to the jaws of a red piranha plant that uncharacteristically rose from a pipe that I was already standing on—a platform that in *Super Mario Bros.* had always been safe.

As I continued to play, I found that *Super Mario Bros. 2* asked me again and again to take a leap of faith and that each of those leaps resulted in my immediate death. This was not fun gameplay, it was punishment—*undeserved* punishment.

I put down my controller, astonished that Mr. Miyamoto had chosen to design such a painful game. It was only later that I came to understand that Mr. Miyamoto had handed off most of the design responsibility of *Super Mario Bros. 2* to other Nintendo staff. Apparently, during the year prior to the Japanese release of *Super Mario Bros. 2*, Mr. Miyamoto had focused most of his energies on the design of future hit *The Legend of Zelda*.

Amazed at how dark and punishing the supposedly entertaining *Super Mario Bros. 2* was, I immediately shared my thoughts with Mr. Arakawa. In his typical stoic manner, Mr. Arakawa simply acknowledged my comments. By this time, I was well aware of the cultural differences within Nintendo that made bad news known but rarely discussed.

It may seem strange, but in the spring of 1986, *Super Mario Bros.* was no longer the franchise to watch to those inside Nintendo. Mr. Miyamoto's *The Legend of Zelda* had launched in Japan on Famicom in February and was experiencing great success. *Zelda* is an incredibly deep and engaging game. So engaging that I managed to successfully complete it even though all the in-game hints and directions were in Japanese script Hiragana and Katakana—text that I could not read or understand. By the time *Super Mario Bros. 2* crossed my desk, I had already completed *The Legend of Zelda* and was lobbying hard for its quick release in the US.

It wasn't until 1988 that a new version of *Super Mario Bros. 2* arrived on my desk. I immediately recognized it as a remake of a Famicom game that I had reviewed the previous year. I found the new *Super Mario Bros. 2* to be a lot of fun and I told Mr. A so. The rest, as they say, is history.

This book provides a great service by documenting in engaging detail a period in history that meant so much to so many of us. As I read this book, I was reminded of the wonder of playing classic video games. Players will understand and remember fondly the nuanced aspects of gameplay that Jon Irwin describes.

While many have written about the video games of the 80s, no one has previously captured with such a keen eye the pixel-level detail of a game from that era. Irwin has created a rich period piece that accurately describes what happened to *Super Mario Bros. 2* and why. At the same time, he has captured the magic of what it was like to be a kid playing video games when Nintendo and Super Mario ruled the world.

Howard Phillips
Summer 2014

Playing a Mario game is about finding secrets. There may be obvious rewards—a flagpole awaiting a well-timed jump, or some floating star to nab, or the sheer joy of moving gracefully through designed space—but the guts of a great Mario game reside elsewhere, tucked away within the scenery. To uncover that which remains hidden: This is the Mario player's true goal.

Such secrets abound. Their presence tantalizes, buried under the surface, its scent seeping through pixelated bricks. Defeating the final villain is the usual climax; grabbing coins is an ever-present dripfeed of adrenaline. But go back and look more closely. Discover that hidden enclave. Unearth a fount of extra lives. Duck beneath the ground and find yourself in another world. Each moment brings with it a feeling—that ping of bright surprise or smooth warmth of elation—that makes you play and play again.

What happens then, when instead of lying behind coded architecture, a game's best secret is the story of the game itself?

PART I: HEART-POUNDING PANIC

I screamed and ran to smash my favorite slot machine…

—David Bowie

1.

HE IS IMMORTAL. A SHAPE-SHIFTER, a workaholic. Possible misanthrope. His interests are many: virology, golfing, the Olympiad. He exists on shirts, wall decals, baseball caps, backpacks, notepad doodles. Millions of strangers can hum the melody to the soundtrack of his life. Millions more control his chubby body in one of hundreds of video games bearing his likeness and name: Mario.

I'm writing this at my desk in Medford, Massachusetts, a town outside of Boston where I live and work. I am 32 years old. I just celebrated my one-year wedding anniversary with a lovely girl from Pennsylvania. On my desk is a small paper calendar turned to the present month, June. There flies Mario, spreading his Squirrel Suit wings as first seen in *New Super Mario Bros. U*, a game released in 2012 for Nintendo's latest video game home console, the Wii U. I turn my head left: On a small shelf sits a cartridge for *Mario vs. Donkey Kong*, a 2004 game for Nintendo's handheld system Game Boy Advance. Below this is a Super Nintendo, the company's 16-bit console released in 1991, *Super Mario World* in the slot waiting to be powered on.

If I walk out my bedroom door and turn right, I'll see the wall of our dining room stuck with life-size pixilated stickers from *Super Mario Bros.,* the original side-scrolling game from 1985 that galvanized a company's fortunes and an entire industry's flagging momentum. Swivel 180 degrees, step through our living area and enter a side room we call "The Nook." You'll see a board game from Milton Bradley based on *Donkey Kong*; on the cover the titular ape hoists a barrel above his head while a familiar mustachioed man wearing white gloves and red overalls climbs a ladder toward the upright beast. Printed on the side of the box is the arcade game's copyright date, 1981, the year Mario was born.

To Nintendo, Japanese maker of games and toys for more than 100 years, Mario is their philosophy made whole. It doesn't matter what you look like, or how powerful or fast or sexy you are. The packaging is an afterthought. All that counts is your smiling face, and your fingers, bent and aching, trying to perfect that chasm-crossing jump.

That Mario is the protagonist of anything is, frankly, bizarre—the kind of happy accident resulting from a mistakenly checked box or an outbreak in the Game Character wing. Our hero is a fat plumber with a limited wardrobe of overalls and an initialed cap, like a baby wearing a nametag. He speaks in high-pitched bursts of nonsense. His most violent acts expose a not-undue detestation of mushrooms and lizards. Motor skills advanced at a rapid pace, while language has remained somewhat under-developed. But his worth goes far beyond pronouncement of a *Wa-hoo!* or two.

Born into a medium so often depicting the gratuitous sniping of heads, this guileless, lumpy, somewhat pathetic caricature of a caricature has somehow remained not only relevant but the de facto mascot of an entire industry. When we see his face, we think of video games. (To those born after 2000, perhaps that mantle will belong to an Angry avian, or the reflective shield of *Halo*'s Master Chief; I shall weep for you privately.)

And yet in the history of his dominance there remains a strange blip. A game where, instead of kicking turtles and jumping at question blocks, he dug up turnips and raced floating masks. A game where Mario let others steal his limelight. A game allowing seven-year-olds their first pull of a slot machine. And whose magazine cover clay image launched millions into literate pubescence.

A game called *Super Mario Bros. 2.*

2.

MARIO BEGAN LIKE MOST OF US: anonymous and afraid.

His debut came as the unnamed protagonist of *Donkey Kong*, Nintendo's first major success in America. Colloquially termed "Jumpman," he climbed steel girders, leapt over barrels, and wielded hammers. Even before being given the title role, Mario's games proved influential.

Pre-*Donkey Kong*, video games were largely stationary. Spots of light flashed and moved on the screen, but the screen itself held still. Most early arcade games like *Space Invaders* and *Pac-Man* were single-screen experiences. Technology and memory limitations of the time prevented grand playfields extending beyond the boundaries of your monitor. Moreover, subsequent levels were often remixes of the first, with faster enemies or more complicated obstacles. When *Donkey Kong* arrived in 1981, and the ape kidnapper climbed a ladder to the top of his skyscraper cross-section, stomping girders into broken diagonals, he broke the expectation for games to stay in one place.[1]

---

1   *Gorf* was technically first, but come on.

Each screen brings an entirely new environment for Mario/Jumpman to move through. When we think of *Donkey Kong*, most of us think of that first stage—with rolling barrels and a flaming oil drum—but that was only one-quarter of the full experience. Stage Two introduces conveyer belts rolling what look like pies into a furnace. Stage Three involves rising elevator platforms and a possessed hopping spring. The final stage has you removing rivets to dismantle the structure on which Mr. Kong stands; ultimately he falls on his head and you get the girl. That is, until the stages loop and you're thrown right back into the barrel-jumping business.

The entire game is about getting to the top of the screen, where a trapped damsel, Pauline, is held captive, and sending Kong tumbling down. Even interstitial screens represent the climb's progression; the second level is shown as "50 M," meaning fifty meters up, the third level is "75 M," and so on. To rise is to win. Staying put on the ground gets you nowhere.

Once Mario becomes the titular hero, however, expectations shift. For his first starring role, an arcade game simply called *Mario Bros.*, he is given the arbitrary job of plumber; your task is to clean out the sewers under New York City. Technology circa 1983 rendered this dirty job into a series of screens with three levels of platforms. On the top-right and -left side of the screen is a green pipe, out of which stream turtles and crabs, the same sad pets flushed down many a metropolis toilet. As Mario (or his green-outfitted brother, Luigi), you clear out each level by jumping and punching the oddly flexible platform underneath the creatures as they walk, popping the poor thing on their backs. You then run up to the helpless invertebrates and kick them dead.

The frantic pace and inventive locale was a hit with the quarter-shoving crowds. But *Mario Bros.* was a progeny of *Pac-Man* and, indeed, *Donkey Kong*, in that the same basic layout remained throughout. For Mario to become Super, he had to climb out of the sewer and onto the streets.

Super Mario Bros. was less a sequel than it was a reimagining. What if Mario wasn't a lowly plumber stuck in the greasy undergrowth of Brooklyn but a peerless hero, destined to save the inhabitants of a fantastical Mushroom Kingdom? While both *Donkey Kong* and *Mario Bros.* were exercises in climbing up and down vertical shafts, *Super Mario Bros.* is a largely horizontal affair. You run up to a waddling mushroom and stomp on it with a satisfying *thwomp*. You jump underneath glowing boxes suspended in air and are rewarded with coins, the accumulation of which gives you an extra life, possibly an in-joke to bill-paying parents. (Nintendo was the proto-Pixar, layering childish fantasy with subtle cues visible to observant adults.)

Your goal is simple: Run to the right until you can run no longer. Ostensibly, you are on a quest to save a princess. Mechanically, the challenge is in evading moving obstacles and mastering this strange terrain by way of well-timed leaps and combination stomps. At their core, all past and present Super Mario titles have one thing in common: Even the basic act of moving through the game-world feels good, satisfying. Mario has a momentum that feels somewhat *realistic*, insofar as a rotund dwarf in overalls can leap off the back of a walking turtle with any semblance of realism. When you pick up the controller and press this cross-shaped directional pad (D-pad) to the right, your little avatar moves in a way that feels natural and engrossing.

As you move through these hilly lands, besting your adversaries with a kicked shell or flung fireball, you uncover places beyond your assumed limits. Anything above or below the main screen remains hidden until stumbled upon, an alternative path or a room full of bonus coins. When you knock an invisible block and a giant vine sprouts skyward, you climb up, excited and uncertain. You walk on clouds gathering treasure only to inevitably fall back to earth.

If there is one reason Mario games retain their popularity nearly 30 years after their initial debut, it is not due to increasing visual fidelity or a rich narrative, but because the simplest act of video game play—to move an object on a screen—remains uniquely satisfying. That such sorcery takes root in front of a computer at the hands of mere programmers is one of the modern miracles of the Computer Age, alongside Deep Blue's besting of Gary Kasparov at chess, the interconnected threads of hypertext transfer protocol, and Mr. Coffee's programmable self-brewing clock.

Super Mario Bros. 2 lives somewhere in between Mario's prior excursions. His second major game released in the West is, by contrast to the first, a vertical experience. This becomes clear the first moment you take control. In what may be the most memorable opening in the 8-bit canon, you select your character and are immediately dropped from some indeterminate door in the sky. You are now falling through the air. Whereas *Super Mario Bros.* places you on foot for your initial encounter with a slow-moving mushroom creature called a Goomba, *SMB2* makes you plummet to the earth like a tossed action figure out a third-story window. In some ways, this opening scene is the inverse of Mario's first with Donkey Kong;

before moving on, you must first descend and arrive on the ground floor. Another door awaits. You open it and step inside.

3.

CHRISTMAS, 1988. My parents, siblings and I arrive at my Uncle Ronnie's for the holiday. He greets me as he always does, grabbing my tiny seven-year-old palm and pumping it with a ferocity befitting the murder of small rodents. I cackle and hang on with two hands. In the kitchen, my grandmother pours off the cooking water from her mashed potatoes and heats the base for her famous gravy. Elsewhere, the secret ingredient is another vegetable: turnips.

Soon I'm staring at a flickering screen. My cousin Shawn grips the NES control pad hard, willing an extra inch of jump height with an upward thrust of the controller. Smiling cacti with heads stalk the dunes. Shawn plucks a purple veggie from the ground and tosses it into the prickly face. The head falls to the ground. Horrifyingly, hilariously, the next-highest segment grows a wicked grin.

I sit and watch for hours, never playing. I'm not ready. Still, the box alone is wonder enough: Mario, fleshed out as it were, drawn in full-cartoon mustachioed glory. "Mario Madness!" the box promises. The title character is shown mid-jump, holding a turnip. I don't remember turnips in the first one.

The original *Super Mario Bros.*'s box showcased actual game graphics—our hero then was 4374 pixels of various hues. But the picture on *SMB2*'s box reveals white gloves, yellow buttons, brown shoes. Mario's eyes are dilated, his teeth a thick row of unsegmented white. Strangely, the blue shirt and red overalls of the cover are swapped in-game; your controllable character wears a red shirt and blue overalls. No matter. Unknown to me then, this box art image would form a new starting point for Nintendo's mascot that still lingers today, and remains the baseline in millions of children's heads for how Mario should look.

My older brother Todd had turned thirteen that year. For my brother, Mario became an old habit quickly dropped, just another action figure tossed in a bin somewhere, forgotten atop an impressive collection of G.I. Joes and other childish things.

I bore the brunt of his flagging attentions. Our NES was his, after all. I did not play *Super Mario Bros. 2* until years later. When I finally did, this is what I saw:

The opening screen promises something out of vaudeville or a silent film. A red frame surrounds a vibrant sky-blue backdrop with the words

SUPER
MARIO BROS
2

set in a shadowed blocky font. Surrounding the frame is a tableau of characters, their actions frozen, the moment washed out in the sepia hue of aging paper. The scene acts as a flash-forward into the game's odd action: Luigi holds up some creature, its stout body mid-wriggle and upended, its tiny legs skyward. Toad has just thrown what looks like a turnip with eyebrows. Some aberration of nature, an enrobed squat thing with its face hidden behind a blank white mask, lumbers toward Luigi, presumably to save his friend. And there on the right side of the screen stand Mario and Princess Toadstool, the former not rescuing the latter but instead both facing the action, ready to jump in.

Press start and the game's theatrical promise is proven out. Red curtains surround the four heroes, now standing at attention, bleached into grayscale and looking out at the player. Push a hovering yellow arrow left or right and each character blooms into color for the first time. The screen instructs you in white text on a black background: "Please select player." The grammar is uncertain; are we to select the character with which we will play? Or is there a missing comma, and we, the player, are advised to select?

When you press A and your chosen character raises his or her hand, you've enacted a choice more akin to picking members of a kickball team than saving the world. *Super Mario Bros.* begins with you as Mario, dropped into a place you are expected to explore. You and Mario are the same. In the sequel, the game addresses you directly. You are instructed to take part. Games were growing slightly more nuanced in their interactivity. The developers were talking to us, the players, even if only in the most rudimentary of ways. Those curtains were no toss-away detail: To push the A button was to pull the curtain up and begin this fabricated adventure. We were the audience and performers, both.

And what a strange performance.

After you, as Mario (or Luigi) (or Toad) (or Princess Toadstool), fall out of the sky and walk though that door on the ground, you enter a strange land of palm trees and circular clouds. Wind perpetually blows to the east; small tufts of red grass wave in this direction, and when you pluck one from the ground you produce a vegetable. There's a Chekhovian logic to video games: If given something to hold, you must throw it at an enemy. Sure enough, a small tottering foe pursues you at a tortoise's pace. The masked creature from the title screen has found you. You do not wish to see this mobile blob, horrific in its vague girth, any longer. And so you chuck whatever projectile is at hand: in this case, what looks to be a smiling turnip. If your aim is true this enemy, which you'll come to know as "Shyguy," flips upside-down, defeated by fresh produce.

This first encounter teaches you that *SMB2*, then, will not follow the same guidelines as its predecessor. In *Super Mario Bros.*'s first level, World 1-1, you walk up to a waddling mushroom-like figure. The body appears vulnerable, a squishiness hinted at by the creature's already misshapen head. You jump upon the Goomba and sure enough, it flattens into oblivion.

Indeed, this maxim—To Defeat Your Enemies, Jump On Them—is one of the many Mario Rules that have been chiseled into the standard instructions of a player's mind in the 30 years hence.[2] The second enemy you encounter, the shell-topped Koopa Troopa, demands a similar if more involved tactic. Jump on the turtle and it hides within its shell home. From there you can kick, ignore, or eventually pick the shell up and heave the projectile as you wish. But most attacks begin with the humble jump.

Super Mario Bros. 2 subverts this expectation. That first enemy you spy, the strange, sad Shyguy, resembles the Goomba in that both comes across as harmless, an easy opponent on which to learn the ropes.

---

2   Hold the Run Button and Do Not Let Go; Flee All Fire But Your Own; Swimming is Hard and Only Worth it for the Music; Lakitu the Cloudrider is a Pestering Nuisance and Must be Dethroned, et cetera.

If you choose not to pick up your veggie-projectile, you will most likely jump upon the Shyguy and expect a satisfying smoosh. Not so. Instead our friend continues on his path, unaffected and oblivious to his new passenger, for Mario is now standing on this creature's head, along for the ride.

First-timers must be confused. *What now?* To jump upon what seems to be an enemy and have it ignore you, neither attack you in return or be harmed in any way, is to bite into an orange and taste nothing. This is something you've done countless times, yet now, unannounced, the rules have changed.

Through acquired playground wisdom or a quick glance at the manual, you soon learn what to do. Press the B Button while atop your foe and *voilà*—you scoop it up, your transporter now held aloft like a baby being calmed, and carry the poor thing until another approaches. Then, in a moment of Darwinistic survival, launch this lesser-than creature toward its kin, one battering the other, and watch as they fall in front of the gameworld's boundaries and below the screen, into whatever doomed blackness exists there, swallowed and forgotten.

The rest of the level provides a peek at the game's machinery, hinting at its slapdash origins. Find and throw a POW block—a symbol from the first *Mario Bros.*—and all on-screen enemies are defeated. Pluck the fourth tuft of grass on the first tall platform and, behold, a magic potion that when thrown opens a door to a silhouette world playing a familiar tune. Snag enough cherries and a flashing star floats up lazily from the bottom of the screen, granting you invincibility and the same frantic staccato two-note beat ingrained in your skull from playing *Super Mario Bros.* Later, when you pluck a key off the ground and a theatrical mask comes to life and chases you with the staggering acceleration of a drunk bird of prey, you will scream and throw the key into quicksand and only then will that evil thing ignore you. For now.

In 1988, we didn't know any better. The name on the box is Mario's. Of course there are invincibility stars! Of course there are 1-Ups. But then why does the story in the instruction manual call this place 'Subcon, the land of dreams' and not the Mushroom Kingdom? Where are those floating question blocks? Why can't I fling fireballs from my hands? By the end of the first level, when, instead of leaping onto a flagpole, you encounter a bowl-mouthed, egg-spitting lizard, the nation's children should have gathered their collective wits and thought: Something smells Cheep-Cheepy.

There was a reason this game was called *Super Mario Bros. 2* but, in fact, did not look or sound quite like a *Super Mario* game. To receive an answer requires the presence of a question. And at the time of its release, nobody even knew there was a question in the first place.

Reviews at the time certainly treated the game as a direct successor. Julian Rignall's July 1989 review in the British magazine *Computer + Video Games* begins, "Question: How do you follow-up a game that's considered by many to be one of *the* all-time classic video games… Answer: You just take the basic gameplay and improve it!" Rignall gives *SMB2* high marks, rating the game at 97% and calling it "a stunning sequel which oozes class and playability." He caps off the review with a veiled threat amongst the hyperbole: "The best Nintendo game yet released—miss it at your peril."

Major entertainment publications did not cover games back then. They were still relatively new, considered by many in the old media guard as youthful pursuits, as unworthy of critical attention as shooting squirrels with BB guns or underage sips of Dad's Jack Daniels. One of the only other reviews published at the time was in the October 1988 issue of *Computer Entertainer*. The magazine itself was a sideline run by two sisters who worked as Warner Bros. music executives.[3] A decade before Napster, these sisters had an inkling digital entertainment would be huge, but

---

3   One was allegedly Prince's manager, years before The Artist's infamous fallout with the label.

their vision was ahead of its time; the magazine folded before the 90s even began. But not before calling *SMB2* "a sequel that's every bit as entertaining as the original game." The review ends with odd emphasis: "<u>Nintendo</u> does it again."

What they had done, in fact, was not apparent to any of us in the English-speaking, game-playing public. But to realize how this now-classic came to be, we first have to uncover a game that came out two years earlier, released in Japan only, with a very curious title: *Super Mario Bros. 2.*

4.

IN 1986, NINTENDO RELEASED their new Nintendo Entertainment System across the Western world after a brief test-run in New York the previous winter. Back in Kyoto, the Mario machine continued to crank. Now that his first starring role was a smash, a team of developers was looking to satiate the growing demand for two-dimensional running and jumping. Shigeru Miyamoto, creator of *Donkey Kong* and *Super Mario* himself, was busy on other projects, including an exploratory adventure game called *The Legend of Zelda* and an unnamed vertical-scrolling prototype. So the assistant director of *Super Mario Bros.*, Takashi Tezuka, was given the keys to the Mushroom Kingdom. Tezuka understood that Japanese gamers were a quick learn: The first *SMB.* had already been dissected and mastered. Veteran players needed something tougher to chew on.

Tezuka was 25 and a fan of fantasy tomes such as *The Lord of the Rings*. A large aspect of Tolkien's novels was "the arduous journey." Just as Homer's words punished Odysseus, pushing him through task after ignoble task just to prove his mettle and get back to his true love, so did the fantasy author seem to nudge his hobbits and elves down the more challenging path, just to see how far he could take them. Tezuka no doubt soaked up such sadistic tendencies.

Sūpā Mario Burazāzu 2, or *Super Mario Bros. 2,* came out in Japan on June 3, 1986 for the Famicom Disk System. At a glance, the game looks the same as *Mario 1*: the same blue sky, the same brown bricks suspended in air, and the same scuttling mushrooms and bouncing winged turtles and flagpoles. This imaginary land still lay riddled with secrets. Items (power-ups, in the parlance of games) are still locked away in shining blocks endorsed with a glowing question mark. No one asks who put these blocks there and how; they are there, and that is enough.

The first hint of foul play in *Super Mario Bros. 2* appears when you, playing as either Mario or Luigi, leap up to pound one of these question blocks with what looks to be his head but, upon closer investigation, is an out-stretched hand balled in a fist. A Power-Up mushroom emerges, gliding along the ground as if coated in ball bearings. Having played *Super Mario Bros.,* you know this mushroom to be good; eating it (or simply touching it, as we never see Mario consume the thing) provides a sudden spurt of growth. Think Popeye with his spinach, or a Gummy Bears with its eponymous juice, or Barry Bonds with a smear of anabolic cream.

So you follow after this mushroom. And at the moment of contact you finally notice the signs, seconds too late, that something is wrong. This mushroom looks ill. Whereas all mushrooms that sprouted from question blocks in *Super Mario Bros.* were bright orange and yellow, the same autumnal color of the question blocks themselves, this mushroom in *Super Mario Bros. 2* is a sickly purple. It appears to be desiccated, its skin the pallid hue of a bloated corpse. You soon learn the result of capturing this power-up is not power but death. Your tiny man stops, mid-air, peering out at the screen, legs akimbo, and then falls down, sliding not below the ground, as we one day will, but in front of it—one of the many reminders that this is no simulation of living but a world built for play and challenge, one with only a passing interest in the laws of nature.

You have done what you thought the game wanted you to do—hit a shiny block and grab the power-up—and the game has killed you for it. Welcome to the original *Super Mario Bros. 2*.

•

The Japanese *Super Mario Bros. 2* was hard. Nails-from-diamonds hard. Organic Chemistry hard. "Call your doctor if it lasts four hours" hard. Tezuka took the formula established in *Super Mario Bros.* and did not build on it so much as construct a series of hateful booby-traps masquerading as levels.

Gaps in the floor that required precision timing in the first game now also required luck; gusts of wind could push you off-course if you jumped too early or too late. Whereas the first game was winnable without unlocking a single secret, certain areas in *Super Mario Bros. 2* could only be passed by finding an invisible brick hiding in the air, providing the necessary foothold for another leap of faith.

Nintendo was not coy in demonstrating the game's brutality. A commercial touting its release showed gameplay footage of one such dastardly moment. Mario leaps from a trio of narrow platforms across a chasm toward the end-of-level flagpole. In order to reach the pole he must first jump on a Bullet Bill, that arm-flexing ammunition from the original game, flying across the sky. But the sequence is too taxing; the player's momentum falters and Mario plummets into a pit.

The next moment a cartoon Mario hangs from atop the screen, as if grabbing onto your television has saved him from certain death. A bandage covers a forehead wound. A single tear drops from his eye. He turns to the viewer and says, "*Hetakuso!*" a phrase that means, "You're hopeless," or literally, "Unskilled crap." The commercial cuts back to the player, a young Japanese girl with bangs and a pink ribbon in her hair. She shakes the controller and yells fiercely at the screen: No translation needed.

To the masochists among the Japanese game-playing public, this new Mario was the ultimate test of your time-honed skills. Bi-weekly game magazine *Famicom Tsushin* named *Super Mario Bros. 2* their number one game a month after its release. Though it never sold as well as the original phenomenon, Japanese tills rang up over two million copies, a remarkable feat given the limited success of the Disk System itself.

But even the native audience couldn't trouble themselves with clearing such devious levels. A strategy guide for the original *Super Mario Bros.* published by Tokuma Shoten was a number one bestseller in both 1985 and 1986, topping popular novels and manga titles. The same publisher's guide for *Super Mario Bros. 2* did not crack the top 30 the year of its release. Later, when the game would finally cross the ocean as an unlockable bonus in a Game Boy Color port of the original, its retrofit title explained what that simple numeral could not. This was *Super Mario Bros.: For Super Players.* Tezuka's taunt barely eked out acceptance in his homeland. His vision would prove even more trying in the West, its population so used to winning.

•

Howard Phillips was one of the first employees at Nintendo of America (NOA), the fifth on the payroll. During the company's mad scramble to get *Donkey Kong* machines into bars and arcades, they hired Phillips to work in the warehouse as a stock boy. His duties soon outgrew his label. He not only organized machines for delivery and storage but set to work replacing the necessary circuit boards that turned the flagging *Radar Scope* into *Donkey Kong*. As the American division geared up to bring Nintendo's successful Famicom over to the West, Phillips's skills at not only moving games but playing them became a valuable asset.

By 1985 he was helping evaluate Japanese games as potential products to bring over for the newly christened Nintendo Entertainment System (NES). He was no executive, just a kid who knew what he liked and why he liked it. He became the filter between East and West; since most development was done in Japan, titles needed to be translated and deemed suitable for another culture. They also had to be fun.

This last, most important criterion was Phillip's strong suit. The president of NOA, Minoru Arakawa, trusted Phillip's insights into what made for a good game. He would play the latest in-development games from Japan and send notes to his boss. A positive review might spark a decision to bring the title over. A negative one could keep a game from ever crossing the ocean.

For a guy who started in the stock room, Phillips now wielded tremendous power within a multi-million dollar Japanese company and its American arm.

When the sequel to *Super Mario Bros.* landed on his desk, he tore in expectantly. Anticipating filet mignon, he bit into gristle. Where *SMB* was joyous and full of secrets, this *SMB2* mocked you for playing and punished you for exploring. Warp pipes, much ballyhooed in the original for boosting you past entire worlds, now sent you back to the beginning of the game. Somewhere, Tezuka was laughing. Phillips was not.

"Not having fun is bad when you're selling fun," Phillips, now the founder of his own consulting firm, said in a 2012 interview on The Nerdist podcast. Later, he'd write about the frustrating experience: "Few games were more stymieing than *Super Mario 2* on Famicom." It took a player's confidence away, decimating self-worth. He knew the American public would not take kindly to this specific brand of punishment.

Games on the NES were infamously difficult; the phrase "Nintendo Hard" has come to describe modern games that approximate the sheer brutality of 8-bit design from this era. But hard is one thing; unfair is another. To release a game that taunted and enflamed the way the Japanese *Super Mario Bros. 2* did would taint the good name of a historic success.

Besides, in 1987, the year after Phillips first saw and evaluated the Japanese sequel, people weren't in the mood for dour cultural experiences. On October 19 of that year, the stock markets crashed and the Dow Jones lost over 500 points in one day. The Space Shuttle Challenger tragedy the previous winter still hung in the air, a pall over the country's optimistic pursuit of progress. Top-grossing films narrowed complex realities into easy entertainment: *Good Morning, Vietnam* framed the disastrous war as a comedy vehicle for Robin Williams just as the continued expansion of women into the workplace was boiled down into *Three Men and a Baby*. This was not a landscape into which Mario, holding a shaving cream pie behind his back and a hand-buzzer in his cupped palm, would be well-received.

The propulsive launch of the NES, spurred by the pack-in sensation *Super Mario Bros.*, was finally ebbing back into normalcy. Nintendo of America needed to keep the momentum going. They needed Mario. Just not the one they were given.

5.

HIROSHI YAMAUCHI WAS THE THIRD president of Nintendo Company Limited (NCL), a company over a century old. Famously irascible, the man ruled Nintendo on instinct and could crush a game-maker's hopes with a cold stare. But he was not only Arakawa's boss—he was also his father-in-law. And now Arakawa, on the hunch of an American kid, had to call him up and say that this new Mario game was not good enough.

No transcript of this phone call exists. No meeting notes are publically available. Not only does Nintendo build secrets into their games, the company itself runs like a level from a Mario game, all hidden doors and inaccessible treasures. The full-color story of what happened next still remains locked up in some file cabinet, tucked away in Nintendo's headquarters in Kyoto. But we know this much: It all began with a dream.

•

In the summer of 1987, the Dream Factory opened for business.

Fuji Television is a major Japanese TV station, operating multiple networks that focus on sports, news, and drama. Broadcasting began in 1959. Nearly 30 years later, to drum up viewership and raise awareness of the company's content, they decided to hold a summer-long event called Yume Kōjō, or "Dream Factory."

Celebrities manned phone booths during telethons. Singing competitions took place, a precursor to today's omnipresent reality shows. Many Japanese companies sponsored the proceedings. Fuji even commissioned a video game starring the official mascots of the festival.

And so Nintendo, a few years into their success with the Famicom, was tasked with making a game for the event. Fuji gave them a set of characters to work with, clothed in Arab garb and called the Imagine Family. From this minimal direction, Nintendo's team created a bizarre adventure of flying carpets, thrown produce, slinking snakes, walking cacti, and irritable masks. They called it *Yume Kōjō: Doki Doki Panic*. "Doki Doki" is an onomatopoeia term for a beating heart. The subtitle, then, can be translated as "Heart-Pounding Panic."

The same physical condition might describe the feeling of two developers as they worked on what would become this game deep within Nintendo's opaque walls. An early, in utero version of *Panic* began as a follow-up to their most successful yet: They were experimenting with a new *Super Mario Bros.* game. This one, however, would pay homage to the past, placing the goal not far down a horizontal path, but at the top of the level, just like *Donkey Kong*. Only this time, the world would extend beyond the top of the screen. Secret areas of *Super Mario Bros.* existed above the clouds, but were rare and a single level above the main path. This new game would continually ascend, mirroring this company's confidence after a century of finding its way.

But when Shigeru Miyamoto and a young developer named Kensuke Tanabe looked at this prototype, they felt something was off. Two characters stacked blocks on top of each other to progress ever-upward, but the screen only moved in single jarring swoops, shifting up once you approached the top, so that you'd begin again near the bottom.

Nintendo had just released their add-on to the Famicom called the Disk System, an add-on to the original Famicom that used rewritable diskettes instead of cartridges. But the system had not proven as popular as its forebear. What was thought a strength—the format allowed games to be erased and rewritten onto the same diskette, allowing players to visit a store kiosk and select from a rotating choice of the newest titles—became burdensome to casual customers and problematic to collectors. And *Super Mario Bros. 2* was not the system-seller the original had been. Teams were on a fast track to write intriguing new software to help the system gain a foothold.

Developers were still learning the new hardware; this prototype had not been optimized fully, its code not efficient enough to render images in the same smooth, scrolling fashion as *Super Mario Bros.* And the gameplay just wasn't that much fun. Miyamoto stopped the project before it could continue longer. But he gave young Tanabe an idea.

"Make something a little bit more *Mario*-like," Tanabe recalls his boss telling him. The compromise called for a game including horizontal levels such as *SMB*, but smaller sections of this new kind of vertical gameplay. Lifting blocks turned into pulling up vegetables as projectiles. What began as an experiment shifted into an amalgam of past successes with new ideas. The final piece needed was a world, something akin to Mario's Mushroom Kingdom. Abstract mazes or vacuous star systems were no longer compelling environments: The simplicity of *Pac-Man* or *Asteroids* belonged to an earlier era, being pushed out by the stock narratives of wartime or colorful fantasy. This new adventure needed adventurers.

One day in 1987, Tanabe took a meeting at Fuji Television where they handed him a piece of paper with four mascot characters from Yume Kōjō, bedecked in Middle Eastern clothes as if having leapt out of *A Thousand and One Nights*. He remembers being told, "Make a game with this." As a 24-year-old employee having joined Nintendo less than a year prior, he was in no position to argue. The characters' garb inspired the game's premise. While two siblings read a bedtime story, a green three-fingered claw reaches out from the book and pulls the children into its pages. A monkey bystander sees the kidnapping and scurries to tell its owners what happened. Like some lost story from the Persian classic, this family leaps into the book left open on the still-ruffled sheets. With the four characters—the man, his wife, their son, and a young girl—stuck inside the book, the game finally begins.[4]

How such a scenario helps promote a television channel's summertime festival is a curiosity. Perhaps the simple moral was: Books are dangerous; watch more TV! More likely, this was simply Fuji TV trusting their characters in the hands of Nintendo, the *de rigeur* kings of gaming. The chosen storyline and content mattered little to Fuji; now millions of game-players, young and old, were consuming a subtle kind of advertisement.

In Japan, everything was roses. Even on the less popular Famicom Disk System, Nintendo's contract work became a hit. And for good reason; built from the discarded prototype's wreckage, traces of the game hummed with that singular Mario magic. The premier

---

4   Popular culture has revised the relationship between the boy and the girl to that of brother and sister, but the characters were originally conceived of as a boyfriend and girlfriend pair.

game magazine in Japan, *Famitsu* (the retitled *Famicom Tsushin*), gave *Doki Doki Panic* relatively high marks, scoring 31 out of a possible 40. What's most interesting about the critical reception is the repeated comparison made by reviewers to a certain *Super* title. One calls it "an action game that's a slight remix of 'Super Mario'."[5] Another says, "It may SEEM like 'Super Mario,' but it's actually completely different." There was no lack of side-scrolling adventure games back then, yet something about *Panic* registered as having Mario DNA with little onscreen evidence. "This is so incredibly adorable," praises a third critic. The same could not be said for Mario's original sequel, the one with the poisonous mushroom.

And as 1987 rolled on, the American offices searched for another blockbuster to match the swell of attention given to *Super Mario Bros.*

Miyamoto's follow-up, a more complicated quest filled with treasure chests, fairies, and a sword-swinging elf, was about to release in the West with the title *The Legend of Zelda*. But other, non-Nintendo games were finding a receptive audience. A bevy of new games based on familiar tropes came out that year, and with it the modern landscape of action-heavy video games was coming into focus.

---

5   Translated by Clyde Mandelin for LegendsofLocalization.com

Contra turned the jungle warfare of the film *Predator* into a two-dimensional shooting gallery with aliens. *Castlevania* took Universal's famous movie monsters and stuck them in a labyrinthine castle, mere minions of the building's owner, Dracula himself. *Mega Man* introduced American players to the titular character, a blue robot with a cannon for an arm. Millions of boys and girls (and their parents) took control of hero after hero, aiming for that vicarious triumph only available through the skillful manipulation of plastic buttons. Mario's face, once the default image blaring from this grey box infiltrating thousands of new homes each day, slowly faded from screens.

Nintendo of America had seen the Japan-made sequel and demurred. Its poison-soaked mushrooms and sudden windstorms would only irritate a population of wannabe experts. Japanese players thrived on a challenge—the more impossible the better. Americans, perhaps less accustomed historically to the stale taste of defeat, had begun calling into Nintendo's new hotline, asking for tips and tricks at more than $1 a minute. These games were hard. And at $50 a pop, to die ten minutes into the game was not only frustrating but a poor value proposition. The kids of savvy investors saw the despondency on their parents' post-Crash-of-87 faces. They weren't used to this. It was un-American to lose.

Back in Seattle, president Arakawa saw the popularity of these tip hotlines as proof that access to the company's secrets was a viable commodity. As the markets roiled and Nintendo approached their second holiday shopping season in the States, plans began to extend this by-the-minute umbilical cord into something more regularly nourishing. And wouldn't it be great if a certain mascot could pave the way for Nintendo's next big push as a cultural phenomenon? He took over their living rooms. Why not their mailboxes too?

6.

GAIL TILDEN WAS ONE OF the earliest employees at Nintendo of America. She remembers company picnics that were 35 people large. Tilden was a part of the small force that swept through New York City during the holiday season of 1985, getting retailers to sell this new device called the Nintendo Entertainment System, staying after hours to put together cardboard displays introducing R.O.B. the Robot. Over a decade later, she would spearhead the global launch of a Japanese phenomenon called Pocket Monsters. Another ten years after that, as Vice President of Brand Management, she watched as a tiny white box called the Wii and its strange remote-shaped controller exploded in popularity, all due to a game of Tennis and a round of Bowling. But she never would have joined the company at all if she hadn't attended a friend's baby shower.

Her first job out of college in the early 80s was writing about outdoor clothing for Brittania Sportswear, outside of Seattle. Soon after, her boss left, taking a job in nearby Redmond. Each was trying to start a family; they kept in touch. One day, her former employer called her with a question: "Have you ever heard of the game *Donkey Kong*?"

Tilden laughs, recalling the conversation with her slight nasal twang. I had arranged a talk with her about the old days at Nintendo, to try and glean some details about *Super Mario Bros. 2*'s launch in the West. We spoke over Skype. Her still-youthful face glowed blue in the light of her computer monitor over the streaming video connection, eyes peering out behind chunky black glasses. A fishbowl sat empty behind her on a dresser.

"I'm at this Japanese company,'" Tilden remembers her former boss saying. "If you're coming to my baby shower, we could talk about it."

The arcade game starring a then-anonymous Mario was a massive success, its red-and-black upright cabinet a fixture in not only arcades but in taverns and smoky bars across the country. Nintendo was looking to expand. Amongst gifts of tinkling mobiles and a new crib, her old boss invited her to join the team.

Tilden took the job, with a caveat: Her husband had applied to Harvard Business School, and if he got in she would have to leave. "He did not end up getting in, thank goodness for me!" Tilden said. "I stayed at Nintendo."

By 1988 she was Marketing Manager, overseeing the relationship between the company and its fans. She attended mall events, interacting with the public and showing off new titles to clamoring kids and bemused strangers alike. She also attended trade shows, organizing how and what their presence would be. Her modus operandi was advertising, public relations. And she knew the best kind of relations were direct; Tilden orchestrated the mailing out of regular pamphlets, called the *Fun Club News*, to players who filled out registration cards, keeping them up-to-date on Nintendo's latest happenings.

For many young players, the *Fun Club News* was the first printed material they'd ever seen about their new favorite pastime. The free pamphlet was billed as a reward to those who registered their game warranties, but it also worked as a clever initiative to grow player engagement and build a master list of addresses where Nintendo hardware resided. The first four-page newsletter was sent to 700 homes. The mailing list grew exponentially; by early 1988, over one million people received the newsletter. By then, the cost of sending out a free newsletter outweighed the gains.

Arakawa saw the huge success of Japanese magazines devoted to gaming and comic culture in the East. He wanted to bring that same devotion to America. They would turn their newsletter into a subscription-based magazine. Tilden was chosen to lead the operation. And in a move that would send Mario into the homes of Nintendo's legions of fans, Tilden saw to it that everyone who'd signed up for the Fun Club would receive the first issue for free.

•

"When you're in a brand new industry, there's not a lot of history to go on," Tilden told me. "And certainly we weren't trying to be like the people that just imploded the industry."

In 1982, early success of the Atari 2600 led others to cash-in; Mattel started selling their own system, the Intellivision, and the Colecovision soon followed. Any and all games sold. So companies put out more games, skimping on quality. Retail shelves soon became swamped with mediocre product. Interest waned. Stores were forced to sell off overstock at bargain bin prices. Two years before the NES launched in America, all that now remained from the video games explosion was a deep crater.

The Crash of 1983 gave Nintendo a blueprint for what not to do. Don't allow any and every company to put a game on your system. Many Atari games were thinly veiled versions of the same arcade hits. Too much of the same breeds fatigue. In Japan, even though many early Famicom titles were arcade ports, Miyamoto and Gunpei Yokoi made sure to design original, distinct games available nowhere else.

In North America, Tilden and her new boss, Bill White, had to introduce the NES to an American public still wary of videogames, seeing them as a fad that had passed. By 1987, they'd accomplished their mission so well that they now they had to keep up with growing demand. People wanted to know what the best games were. And the best game so far was Mario.

"*Super Mario Bros.* was very successful," Tilden tells me, the phrase an atypical understatement for someone immersed in the selling of products for four decades. "Wanting to keep the marketing machine going, it's my recollection that Mr. Arakawa, [president of] Nintendo of America, asked to put the Mario character family into *Doki Doki Panic* because we wanted to continue the promotion of that very successful franchise."

What began as a Mario prototype, then sublimated into a one-off licensed product for a television partner, became once again a Mario game. *Doki Doki Panic* would be tweaked, reskinned, and sold in North America and Europe as *Super Mario Bros. 2.* Even those in charge of selling the game were, at first, confused.

"It was odd to call it *Super Mario Bros. 2*, since it didn't seem like a sequel to *Super Mario Bros.,*" Tilden acknowledges. But she understood the decision. "[Selling] *Doki Doki Panic* would be reinventing the wheel again in terms of education and marketing push. As opposed to embracing something that people were really loving at the time. *Doki Doki Panic* didn't mean anything to anyone."

But what at first blush seems like an aberration from the series is actually just another in a long line of reinventions for Nintendo's most famous characters.

"If you look at *Donkey Kong 3*, it has nothing to do with *Donkey Kong 1* either," Tilden reminds me. And she's right: The first *DK* is all about Mario/Jumpman, running and jumping on suspended platforms. *Donkey Kong 3* puts you in charge of an entirely separate character, Stanley, who spends the game shooting bug-spray upwards at insects, dislodged by an angry Donkey Kong slapping a hive. And yet that name and number connect the two in some nebulous, ill-described universe. That the sequel in between jettisoned the number two altogether, opting instead for the filial suffix *Jr.*, confuses the issue more.

Donkey Kong itself was a product of business-minded necessity. When Robert Altman's 1980 *Popeye* film brought the cartoon character back into the public eye, Nintendo acquired the license and developed an arcade game in which the plucky title character saves Olive Oyl from the brutish Bluto. The agreement fell apart. Nintendo was stuck with a game and no characters. After some eleventh-hour brainstorming, Miyamoto redrew the kidnapping lout as a giant ape, lengthened and lightened the maiden's hair, and gave the spinach-eating sailor overalls and a mustache. Nintendo's first successful video game was another of their many thoughtful evolutions.

Games were not built to persevere. Their purpose, at least initially, was to *not* last; they were fantastical flights, something loud and compelling to draw your attention (and a few coins out of your pocket). *Space Invaders* was not founded on a deep mythology, nor was it based on a larger, somewhere-out-there world, the way *Star Wars* was. Only in hindsight do we look back and question the utter shift in locale and play style from *Super Mario Bros.* to its translated sequel.

Logic be damned, Arakawa got his wish. A very different *Super Mario Bros. 2* was finally coming to America. Now all they needed to do was spread the word.

PART II: MARIO MADNESS

Leisure-time pursuits will become an increasingly important basis for differences between people...we can anticipate the formation of subcults built around space activity, holography, mind-control, deep-sea diving, submarining, computer gaming, and the like.

—Alvin Toffler

1.

"IT MAY BE THE MOST ADDICTIVE TOY in history," begins Hugh Downs, co-host of ABC news program *20/20*, in an introduction to a feature called "Nuts for Nintendo," highlighting the growing mania over video games and 1988's big holiday titles. Cut to John Stossel, a bushy mustache keeping his face warm on a blustery New York City sidewalk, waiting in line outside an electronics store. His mission? To buy a copy of *Super Mario Bros. 2* for his producer's kid. Nine minutes of interviews with parents and over-the-shoulder video follows, taping kids lying on carpeted living rooms playing Nintendo, their mouths slack. Back in the studio, Barbara Walters asks Stossel a final question: "John, what's your feeling after watching this? Does it make them, you know, braindead?"

Other than the odd mainstream scare story, news and press coverage of games barely existed in the late 80s. Games were sent to stores and put on shelves willy-nilly. Vivid game-boxes appeared at Toys "R" Us or Blockbuster without consumers even knowing how to pronounce some of the titles. Still, through word-of-mouth and blanket advertising, their mindshare grew. And Nintendo ruled.

Back then video games were displayed as plastic cards hung from a wall, each box rendered down into a flat sheet of laminate. On one side was the cover; the opposite side showed the back of the box, screenshots laced with paragraphs about the game's heroes and villains, the struggle of good vs. evil, et cetera—grand annihilations boiled down into pithy copy.

The specifics mattered little. Humans have long been cover-judgers; how was Eve to know that red apple would be anything but succulent and sweet? So, too, did a generation of kids snap up games based on flashy logos or detailed warriors, rich illustration standing in for the game's technical truth: a few chunky blockmen bounding across the same ground colored in six varying hues.

We chose games on gut instinct, pointing at rectangles and crossing our fingers. That you took a slip of paper to a separate counter to actually purchase the game itself should have tipped us off to the transaction being made: This was a lottery. Odds were low you'd win. But we bought those tickets anyway, fingers crossed, eyes gleaming.

And then one day our gaming idol arrived, his mustache rendered in clay.

•

In the summer of 1988, *Nintendo Power* #1 arrived on doorsteps across the country. Its cover announced the impending arrival of something new, something we needed: There was another *Super Mario Bros.* game coming. All at once, thousands of souls opened this glossy magazine, the same shape as their parents' issues of *Time* or *The Economist*, and found what they were looking for.

Games hadn't yet been broadcast in the same pervasive way as other culture. TV ads were fleeting, an occasional shot fired. This magazine, sent out en masse, to be sifted through for 30 days until the next one arrived, was a cluster bomb, a family-friendly blast of nougat-napalm draped over your front stoop. That first issue would eventually be sent to more than 3.2 million homes for free, the highest circulation of any issue for the publication's 24-year history. Soon, *Super Mario Bros. 2* was everywhere, even if nobody knew a thing about it.

The issue is a time capsule of an industry that was still finding its balance. The pages are an amalgam of screenshots, cartoons, and top ten lists. Leafing through the magazine today as a 32-year-old invokes little nostalgia—I was a late subscriber and so never received this in the mail—yet the coverage of *SMB2* reveals both the confidence and the lack of concern for continuity that Nintendo had in its rejiggered sequel.

At just over 100 pages, *Nintendo Power #1* was more the slim and spry Luigi than the stout Mario—subsequent game magazines in the mid-1990s would balloon up to 400 pages long—and *Super Mario Bros. 2* occupied almost a fifth of the entire issue. The first twenty pages of coverage introduced the game, explained basics of play and movement, and concluded with level-by-level tips for beating the first two worlds.

But the first image the new *Power* subscriber saw, the cover, was something else entirely: Mario, posed to mimic the game's box art, in mid-jump with one fist raised and the other around what looks like a carrot, chased by the end boss of the game, a crowned toad named Wart.[6] The two figures traipse over rounded hills, a couple of vegetables stuck in the soil. This tableau was sculpted entirely from clay. An ad agency named Griffes Advertising came up with the idea, plucking inspiration from the then-popular California Raisins, a musical group of anthropomorphic raisins given life through claymation. Mario and Wart wouldn't be singing "I Heard It Through the Grapevine" anytime soon—the cover used a still-photograph of the sculpture, which

6   For some reason, the colors match Mario's in-game sprite (blue overalls, red shirt) instead of the box cover (red overalls, blue shirt).

would live in a fishless aquarium in Tilden's office for years after that first issue went out.

"What was really interesting about it was, first of all, creating Mario in 3D," Tilden said. "There was no 3D Mario." Up until this point, the character lived and died as a two-dimensional image. You either saw a collection of pixels generated by lines of code displayed on a monitor, or you saw a flat drawn cartoon in an instruction manual (or the one jotted down in your school notebook). Until that cover was created, Mario had never been given weight, or the simple curvature of something existing in space. It wouldn't be until 1996 that fans could finally play as a three-dimensional plumber in *Super Mario 64*. This cover image offered a glimpse at the future.

The final pages of *Nintendo Power* #1 complete the indoctrination. An ad shows three teenage boys with *Wonder Years*-era Fred Savage hair and a basset hound flying into the shining beacon of a giant television. One holds a facsimile of this very issue as he enters the screen. Block letters in a courageous purple hue spell out the last word: "Welcome to the vast, exciting new world of *Nintendo Power* magazine." Cue the perforated subscription cards with discount savings off the newsstand price. And in case you'd forgotten, the small print reminds us of all we could have missed: "Just look at the monster review of *Super Mario Bros. 2* in the front of this issue! You'll be a master in no time with all those facts, figures, and detailed action moves at your fingertips."

I asked Tilden if Nintendo considered disclosing the origin of Mario's first big-time sequel. "There was no industry publishing at the time," she said, laughing. "I don't even know who we would have talked to about it." *Nintendo Power* became the first major game-focused publication after the industry's self-induced crumbling. "There wasn't anybody writing anything," Tilden reminded me. "So we could really charter our own path. There was no internet. There was no way for someone else to say, 'Hey, look at this interesting thing Nintendo did.'"

At the time, the word choice—*this interesting thing Nintendo did*—passed me by unscathed. But in rereading our conversation the phrase sticks in my brain.

Until now, I had assumed the decision, to turn this obscure Japanese game into a Mario sequel, was coated with a thin dust of deception. Nobody in the West knew what Nintendo had done. Eventually the lid would be lifted five years hence, in 1993, when a collection of *Mario* NES games sold as *Super Mario All-Stars* for the Super Nintendo included the Japanese *SMB2* newly subtitled *The Lost Levels*. Word spread. A burgeoning World Wide Web allowed those valiant few to connect the dots: Japan's *Doki Doki Panic* had begotten North

America's and Europe's *Super Mario Bros. 2*. Our game was not, in fact, what it had appeared to be.

They lied to us was the immediate, melodramatic reaction. But here is the other, more likely reality. *They did an interesting thing*. This was no yakuza-inspired cover-up. This was the clever manufacturing of something from nothing, an inspired bit of subterfuge.

Consider Nintendo's decision: to reboot a licensed experiment as the next chapter in your tent-pole franchise in the West. What happens if Nintendo's decision fails? If *Super Mario Bros. 2* was not on the cover of *Nintendo Power*, with an instant audience of three million voracious tip-seekers; if the game itself was widely panned as an unworthy successor to the first (an opinion held by some); if the American office didn't convince their Japanese mothership that in order to capture a Western audience they needed something different, something to wow the tube socks off a country of discerning customers already tiring of the last best thing?

For Nintendo fans, the last quarter-century hinges on this game. Yet many dismiss it, shrugging off the oddball world and disparate mechanics as a one-time blip on Mario's peerless catalog. The question remains: What was so interesting about this *interesting thing*?

2.

WHEN I FIRST PICKED UP THE CONTROLLER months ago, returning to this strange off-center Mario game after decades, I'd forgotten much of the experience. Each world I push through rekindles some long-buried moment, a fleeting euphoria or forgotten surprise dredged up from years of layered memories. To play an old game is to deal with personal tectonics; there's both the obstacles on screen and a bank of long-forgotten memories.

There also exists a second dimension normally unseen. As you pull up tufts of grass, revealing vegetables stuck in the ground that now serve as projectiles, you sometimes pull up what looks like a beaker, filled with bubbling liquid. Toss the magic potion on the ground and a door appears. Enter and find yourself in what is known as Sub-space.

Here you can't scroll forward or backward, instead locked into the locale as it appears onscreen. Everything is rendered in silhouette and inverted, this world now backwards below a malevolent purple sky. The only things still in full-color are yourself, the door you came in from, and, if you've chosen wisely, a mushroom that increases your health, invisible from the normal level.

Carry a potion across the level and drop it where you like in the hopes of finding these elusive boosts.

While the mushroom is rare, coins are everywhere in Sub-space, as long as you know what to do. Each time you pull up grass in this shadow reality they become coins, eliciting the same "*ba-ding!*" effect first heard in the *Mario Bros.* arcade game, then made iconic in *Super Mario Bros.* At the end of each level, you spend them to play an end-of-level slot machine game to earn extra lives. Pull up as many coins as you can quickly, though; Sub-space can only be inhabited for a few seconds before you find yourself back where you started.

While most *Super Mario Bros.* games feature a 1-Up system reliant on gathering 100 coins to gain an extra life, *SMB2* sheds that arbitrary reward for this sly nod to the company's gambling past. Defeat the level's last enemy and be whisked away to some interstitial gambling parlor. Three columns of shapes spin and spin. Press A to stop each. Three of a kind grants you one extra life, as does a single cherry in the first column. Two cherries in a row yield two extra lives; three cherries hits the jackpot—five lives.

In the perma-night of Sub-space you earn the right to dabble at the slots, that ubiquitous presence in the perma-day of Las Vegas. But there's more to be found here than coins. Who needs money when you can rend the fabric of space?

•

I'm looking for warp zones.

In the original *Super Mario Bros.*, one famous and well-trod shortcut involves jumping above what appears to be the end of a level and walking, impossibly, across the top of the screen to a hidden space. "Welcome to Warp Zone!" the room says. There await three pipes, each a portal to worlds beyond.

Super Mario Bros. 2 takes the warp zone concept and removes the element of choice. In my original playing of it, some 25 years ago, I never found one of the secret vases that whisk you into a later stage. But now I'm playing more carefully. I'm seeking out nuances I'd initially ignored.

Each world but the last is split into three sections: e.g., the second level of the first world is written World 1-2. I'm playing through World 1-3 now. My health is low; I could use one of those hidden mushrooms. I act on a hunch: I carry a magic potion to the end of the first section of this level, to a place where the scrolling stops and the ground ends in a cliff. Behind me is a door to a large brick structure, leading me to the rest of the level and, eventually, the end boss, a giant mouse named Mouser with Joe Cool sunglasses and a penchant for throwing bombs. On the ground in front of me is a vase about the same height as Mario.

Similar to green pipes in *Super Mario Bros.*, you can enter some of these vases by ducking over top of their opening. Though it's never explicitly explained, you become miniaturized when you enter a vase. The shape of the single room you drop down into is the same shape as the jar, implying you've been transmogrified into some 1/20th version of yourself, in order to scavenge. Sometimes you'll find a key; other times, a single Shyguy, puttering back and forth, its sad existence a cruel decoy.

I toss the potion on the ground beside this jar and enter Sub-space. No mushroom. On a whim I jump on top of the jar and duck. The screen goes entirely black, save for a single line of white letters: "Warp to World 4."

In my apartment bedroom, where I'm playing this on a friend's original Nintendo Entertainment System hooked up to a Sharp 13-inch flat LCD television, I let out a little *whoop!* of surprise. I was not expecting that. I likely knew of this warp at some point in the distant past, but I've been playing like any new player might: experimenting, exploring, looking for treasure. Our cat Sam hears my exclamation as a call of her name; tiptoeing in from the dining room, she soon loses interest and begins knocking down my wife's jewelry onto the carpet and sliding it beneath the bed to horde for later. Her own little pile of coins.

Some 50 ago, a popular Japanese manga named *Doraemon* was first published, about a robotic cat from the future sent back in time to aid a child. He often employed gadgets to help in a certain quest, pulling them out of his "*yojigen*-pocket," which translates to "fourth dimension pocket." One such gadget was the Anywhere Door, through which the user can walk and appear wherever they'd like to go. It's easy to imagine little Shigeru Miyamoto and Kensuke Tanabe, directors of *Super Mario Bros. 1* and *2* respectively, as kids, reading of this futuristic cat robot with its dimensional pockets and warp doors to anywhere. That such devices might find their way into their future video games is no less surprising than George Lucas, years after reading about the Arthurian legend of Camelot, inhabiting his made-up universe with a hero of destiny among a league of knights.

So I've found one warp zone. There are others still hidden away. But since, in the early 21st century, there are no such things as dimensional pockets, nor such inverse reality as Sub-space, the question remains: Where to look?

•

Today I emailed a library at Tufts University about accessing a former student's thesis. The manuscript became a first draft for Chris Kohler's *Power-Up*, one of the few books published focusing on 1980s-era Japanese games. I've read the final version, but I also understand how books come to be: We readers never see the first or second or fifth lines written, only the varnished finale. Might an early chapter, hidden for a decade in the dusty bowels of Tisch Library, unearth some long forgotten detail?

I search online records and find nothing. An archivist emails me back. Digital records for older dissertations are incomplete. Come to the library, they say, and we'll take a look. Ah, but this vase is only a vase: My attempts to locate the thesis, and with it some warp zone into the past, come to naught. Kohler's thesis isn't on site.

Which comes as a surprise to Mr. Kohler when I contact him directly. "I had a copy all printed and bound for them!" he writes in an email. "Whatta buncha jerks." I wouldn't have found much of interest anyway, the author contends. "The good stuff from the paper is in *Power-Up*."

In 2011, Kohler spoke to Tanabe, director of *Panic* and *SMB2,* at the Games Developers Conference, an annual industry meet-up featuring panel discussions, Q & A sessions, and an exposition hall of new, in-development games. Somehow, Kohler cornered the Nintendo veteran into an impromptu reveal: that *Panic* was itself based on a Mario prototype, the first time this was publically discussed.

"I had to drag that *SMB2* conversation out of Tanabe," Kohler told me in an email, "while the PR staff tried to get me back on topic."

Empty-handed, I leave the university's underground stacks, walking down a long narrow hallway. On one side are cabinets filled with papers slathered in dried ink. On the opposing wall are photos of formerly living research: Color reproductions of P.T. Barnum's advertisements featuring Jumbo the Elephant, from which the school's mascot takes its moniker. The 19th century circus maestro gave money to the University to start a Natural History Museum. After the Big Top fell off in popularity, and the museum was all that was left of his legacy, Barnum donated the elephant's massive hide to what was then called Barnum Hall.

In 1975, the museum burned down. All that's left now of Jumbo is a jar of ashes and a displayed trunk. A passing archivist notices my interest. "The trunk on display isn't even Jumbo's," she says. Some other elephant's trunk stands in for the famed pachyderm. Thousands come through the library every year and see an anonymous beast's nose, believing it to be something it's not. Nintendo understands this kind of purposeful mislabeling. Myth is more powerful when the messy sutures of its history are left unseen.

3.

POPULAR OPINION ASCRIBES ONE MAN, a mighty
champion existing far beyond our spectral realm, as
the keeper of the mustachioed one. As time wore on,
many years and games after Shigeru Miyamoto created
Mario for *Donkey Kong*, Nintendo was all-too happy
to promulgate the myth of Miyamoto. He alone could
spin gold coins from a plumber's denim overalls, or so
they said. But of course there were others.

Miyamoto is the wunderkind-turned-producer-
turned-mascot, trotted out at public events as some kind
of game character made flesh, grinning and swinging a
plastic sword. He's one of the few game developers even
named, let alone hailed, by mainstream outlets—the
New Yorker profiled Mario's maker in 2011, while *Time*
listed him as one of the Top 100 influential people in
the world.

Under this immense shadow lurk few other names,
known mostly to an increasingly rabid fan base, fed by
websites and public forums. Most programmers and
coders remain out of sight until a game's final screen
and its scroll of faceless names. Only a few Nintendo
creators are honored, or burdened, with such notoriety:

Tezuka, Eiji Aonuma, Kōji Kondo, Gunpei Yokoi. And even those names are likely unfamiliar to a vast majority of the games-playing public.[7]

Kensuke Tanabe remains largely absent from the narrative. In 1993's *Game Over* by David Sheff—a nonfiction account of Nintendo's history and decades-long expansion into American households—Tanabe is not mentioned once. By that time he'd been working at the company seven years, having directed one of its most popular games.

Tanabe's absence suggests a corporate culture of anonymity; or, rather, one who values group productivity over personal recognition. Since then Tanabe has remained at Nintendo alongside his fellow long-time developers. What little glimpses we're given come from within.

Satoru Iwata is the current President of NCL and Yamauchi's successor. He interviews his development teams on upcoming games and shares these with the public, a kind of journalist-for-the-day reprieve from Iwata's duties. Tanabe features in a number of these

---

7   Aonuma has lead the Zelda franchise since directing *The Legend of Zelda: Majora's Mask* in 2000. Kondo is the famed composer of many Nintendo game scores including titles in the Mario and Zelda franchise, and Yokoi directed early NES hits like *Metroid* and *Kid Icarus* but is most well-known for creating the Game Boy before dying tragically in 1997. More on the latter two soon.

articles, often in a Producer role. These occasional video interviews and promotional images offer clues to who the *Super Mario Bros. 2* director is beyond that sliver of recognition given.

Tanabe speaks softly. He lets his clothes do the shouting, often wearing bright jackets or thoughtful combinations of button-downs and turtlenecks. He has a high-pitched, extended laugh, like marbles being dumped onto concrete. He dyes his hair; promotional videos show dark choppy locks one year, light auburn another. He's been known to wear a choker necklace made of what look like puka shells. He keeps his face clean-shaven but for a faint wisp of five o'clock shadow. His eyebrows are wide but not dense; close observation reveals the perfect lines and surrounding paleness of a wax-job.

Tanabe will be 51 this year. *Doki Doki Panic* and the American *Super Mario Bros. 2* are still the only games he has directed himself. Since then, most of his work has been as something of a Nintendo Ambassador to western studios, proselytizing the Nintendo way to development groups like Retro Studios, an Austin, Texas-based group that has worked on games in the *Metroid* and *Donkey Kong Country* franchises. While most of Nintendo's games are made in Japan, a select few are given to outside companies; they are not given free rein, however, and are in constant contact with the home base in Japan. Tanabe acts as a mediator of sorts, an onsite representative who can help the Western team to both communicate with their Japanese overseers and to better understand what makes a Nintendo game tick.

The first kernel of this work began with the Mario-ification of *Panic*. In a recent interview, Tanabe even refers to his one and only directed project not by its original title, but by the name it would bear in Japan upon its re-release: *Super Mario USA.*

"I have been in the video game business for about 30 years," he says (dubbed into English by a translator at Nintendo of America). "The first game I worked on as a director was..." and here we hear Tanabe pause, an audible "ehhh," not needing any translation. "Well, in Japan it was known as *Super Mario USA.* And it was known as *Super Mario Bros. 2* in America and elsewhere."

This answer is an instructive bit of retconning. The first game he directed was in fact *Doki Doki Panic.* Yet in this promotional video, he all but declares that project to be a footnote, an unmentionable alongside what it would one day be turned into. A faceless entity scrubbed out for its more marketable, charismatic other: This sounds a lot like Tanabe himself.

Tanabe is lesser-known, at least in the West, perhaps due to his work taking on a more collaborative, mediating role. Americans like a leader. One oft-told story is of Miyamoto "upending the tea table," or the

Japanese *chabudai gaeshi,* an expression used to describe a non-negotiable last-minute change. Miyamoto's roles as producer on much of Nintendo's internal development means he constantly oversees the work being done; when he sees something gone wrong, he speaks and they listen.

For instance, a game by the name of *Twinkle Popo* was finished and ready for production. It was thought of as a small project at Nintendo, a diversion for niche audiences. Miyamoto saw potential here, suggesting late-stage tweaks to the game that took the project off the factory line. When it finally released, *Kirby's Dream Land* sold over five million copies and a new beloved character joined Nintendo's ranks.

Though the vocabulary used would differ, I imagine many overturned tea tables in American board meetings. The image smacks of ego and violence, concepts that speak to a populace ruled by presidents carrying big sticks. But stories of Tanabe's involvement resemble a matronly graciousness, more grandmother than Grand Master.

Michael Kelbaugh, then-president and CEO of Retro Studios, told Chris Kohler in 2011 that Tanabe, "is very patient, even at times when he doesn't need to be…and is sincere about teaching Americans, Westerners, the Nintendo philosophy."

Just what is that philosophy, then? One tenet, apparently, is don't give interviews about your philosophy. Repeated requests to Nintendo's PR firm, Golin-Harris, went unanswered as I tried to communicate directly with Tanabe. This was no isolated evasion. Nintendo rarely gives access to journalists writing about their company beyond the standard game review. Jeff Ryan, in the Acknowledgements of *Super Mario: How Nintendo Conquered America*, echoes the lack of access given to him after he explained his project to be a full-scale history of the company.

"Nintendo is a particular company," he writes, "and one of those particularities is not cooperating with the press when it comes to books."

While speaking with Gail Tilden, I asked if she knew of any current employees whom she thought might be willing to speak with me.

"I think you have almost no chance," she said, laughing. "Nintendo does not like to participate in these types of projects because they don't know ultimately how history will be written," she said, adding, "or re-written."

History, as they say, is written by the winners. A company that makes video games creates objects of play to be won by their players. In one sense Nintendo is the ultimate control freak: planner, architect, landlord, all in one. But who runs through these rooms? Who leaps across the chasm, jumps over obstacles, each carefully laid out for the residents' frustration and amusement?

We do. We win the game. Perhaps ownership of the past is not as simple as the maxim suggests. As storytellers have known for eons, the teller herself does not always own her tale.

4.

IN 10TH CENTURY PERSIA, a collection of myths passed down for generations was finally copied down on paper and given the title *Hazar Afsana.* The title translates to "A Thousand Legends." Though now lost, this manuscript is the first known version of what would become *A Thousand and One Nights*, a popular and lasting story cycle still published today, giving life to such tales as Aladdin and his magic lamp, Sinbad's exploits at sea, and the cherubic Ali Baba. All have become a part of both Eastern and Western story tradition.

Doki Doki Panic was influenced by these long-held legends, from the transformative magic lamp and flying carpet to its underground music theme. Much of this made the transition into *Super Mario Bros. 2*. Even the way time works has a Middle Eastern flair.

In the original *Super Mario Bros.*, each stage has a timer that ticks down to zero. Upon reaching a hundred seconds left, a warning trill sounds and the music memorably accelerates, matching your excitable state. When the timer hits zero, Mario dies, as if that ticking clock was a beating heart.

But in both *Panic* and *SMB2*, no such clock winds down, as if in a dream. Time elapses but we, the dreamers, aren't subject to its ticks. One moment we're asleep; the next, we simply wake up.

In the Arabian legend, lovely Scheherazade tells a near-unending sequence of tales to dissuade King Shahryar from making good on his promise—to put to death each member of his harem after spending the night with her. But when visited by this beautiful storyteller who takes care to always end on a cliffhanger, he lets her live for the sake of a satisfying end. Enraptured and insatiable, he listens through all one thousand and one. He eventually not only lets her live but hires scribes to take down her tales for perpetuity—the same book we hold is a creation of its own telling.

The conceit of these tales, known alternatively as *The Arabian Nights*, reminds me of the tale of Nintendo. We, the royal players, are held in their interactive stories' thrall. They keep making them, over and again, for fear of losing our interest. To stave off such inattention, they'll even go so far as to cannibalize their own work to spin another yarn.

Just as Nintendo's characters have blended into the common culture, so have the folk tales found in *A Thousand and One Nights* spread beyond their initial borders. This is a type of culture loaning that Japan and the Americas share: an exotic "other" born outside the confines of each nation's ancestry and brought into the native culture slowly over time, until finally it has become a part of its collective memory. What began as tales shared over centuries ago has evolved to the blunt end-point of Robin Williams voicing a blue animated genie. That's some strange evolution.

Nintendo's *Super Mario 2* switcheroo fits into a much larger tradition of audience misdirection. The story of Aladdin and his lamp, though now published as a part of the *Arabian Nights*, was not a part of the original Arabic, nor was Ali Baba or Sinbad; these stories we know so well were in fact introduced by the translators who brought the tales over to Europe.

The cross-cultural translation of *Doki Doki Panic* into *Super Mario Bros. 2* exemplifies this same human impulse: to make something exotic our own. And by doing so, we sift out much of the unfamiliar and add some of the comforting. Described as such, the act sounds perverse, almost parasitic. And maybe it is. But you can't fault the logic of wanting to swallow down what we can. There's only so much time left.

5.

GAMES BASED ON LICENSED CHARACTERS, such as those found in movies or TV shows, often become something between an advertisement and entertainment, another avenue from which to take a fan's money. Licensed games are also reputed to be quite terrible. This was especially true during the NES years.

Countless examples exist, from *Airwolf*, based on the TV show about an advanced helicopter, to *Yo! Noid*, a 1990 NES game starring the mascot for Domino's Pizza.[8] What happens to your playable character is based on game logic, having as much to do with the property as a child's game of Doctor has with the latest advances in orthopedic oncology.

Friday the 13th on the NES, based on the horror film franchise of the same name, is a laughable slog through cookie-cutter environments and a near-impossible difficulty, with vague clues and a recurring enemy in Jason who kills you almost instantly. "You and your

---

8 *Yo! Noid* is another Westernized game based on a pre-existing Japanese one, with the Noid being retrofitted into *Kamen no Ninja Hanamaru*.

friends are dead," the screen tells you. "Game over." Most players treat this as a blessing.

Unlike in those pop culture tie-ins, the world of *Doki Doki Panic* was created out of necessity; there was no pre-existing show or comic or film—just four mascots with empty histories. The game itself—pulling up veggies, unlocking underground doorways, leaping across waterfalls and whale spouts—was based on this Fuji TV festival the way a cheese sandwich is based on a cow: a most creative of adaptations, using raw material to create something else entirely.

Tanabe and his team had carte blanche to create a world from the ground up without forcing the expected. When *SMB2* was chiseled from the pre-existing *Doki Doki Panic*, most of these characters, backgrounds, and objects remained. But this was a Mario game now, after all. Even with only one full-on adventure under his belt, the plumber's name came with high expectations. And though the NES could only render 25 colors onscreen at one time, the graphics team made sure to use all of them when giving the world of *Super Mario Bros. 2* its Western makeover.

And so vegetable leaves, stationary in *Panic*, now swayed in the breeze. The character select screen turned from a shabby beige line chart in *Panic* to a full-color theater scene with velvet curtains and gold ropes. Though *Panic* introduced the end-of-level slot-machine bonus game, it played out on an all-green background, like an evening news weather update gone wrong; *SMB2*'s slots borrowed the same intricate design from its title screen.

Some changes appear more culturally tinged. *SMB2*'s magic potion, from which you access Subspace, was originally a magic lamp in *Panic*. Dropped on the ground, the lamp breaks into a poof of smoke, revealing the door into an alternate dimension. But hold this new bottled potion and watch tiny bubbles float to the surface; the dropped beaker reacts with the same door-creating explosion. (Perhaps American players were assumed to be more familiar with chemistry experiments gone awry than lamps encasing mystical powers; Disney's *Aladdin* would not come to theatres until 1992, four years after *Super Mario Bros. 2* and its mélange of Middle Eastern tropes.)

So ingrained was Mario's ability to "power-up" and grow bigger in the minds of his players that *SMB2*'s characters grew and shrank where *Panic*'s did not. The visual cue introduced unintended exploits such as standing safely under low-flying enemies; to compensate for the smaller body yet keep the player in danger, the developers increased the size of each character's head.

Another change in keeping with Mario tradition was the ability to run by holding the B button. *Doki Doki Panic*'s family members strolled leisurely. You could only walk. Play *Panic* today and the pace feels inert, plodding. Raise your hand if you play a *Super Mario Bros.* game with your thumb jammed on that run button, never to be lifted except to toss the occasional projectile. The choice to run was an essential change even if running itself was never necessary.

The most notable recurring change from Japanese *Panic* to American *SMB2* is the relative lack of emphasis on masks. Simple-looking blocks used as projectiles or stepping stones were initially small masks in the Japanese game, resembling dramatic moods such as Comedy or Tragedy. The end doorway of each level was also originally a giant mask with its mouth opening wide. Even the Japanese box's cover art featured the young Arabian hero throwing a mask instead of the iconic turnip.

Theatre plays a huge role in Japanese culture, perhaps more so than in America's early history, and is a clear influence here. One particular format called *Nō*, popular from the 14th to 15th centuries, emphasized the use of carved masks, each of the actors wearing them to announce to the audience their primary trait. Mask-carving is seen as an important art in the country's history, also seen in the more widely known works of *kabuki*. But it is the *bunraku*, or puppet theatre, where we see a more direct connection to the world of Mario and Nintendo's cadre of characters.

If any ancient art resembles the magic of game design, it's the wielding of puppets, where men and women hide behind walls, unseen, manipulating fantastical actions onto a constructed personage, all for the delight of an audience with little idea how it all works. Miyamoto himself has confessed a love for puppetry. A long-standing experimental game of his, whispered about for years but never released, was known as *Marionette.*

Donald Keene, one of the world's foremost voices on Japanese culture, has studied and written about Japanese literature for decades. In his book, *The Battles of Coxinga*, he relays the account of a philosopher attending a *bunraku*, dated to the mid-17th century, astonished at what he saw:

> Some leapt about and some rowed boats and sang. Some had been killed in battle, and their heads and bodies were separated. Some were dressed in the clothes of the gentry. Some shot arrows, some waved sticks, and some raised flags or bore aloft parasols. There were dragons, snakes, birds, and foxes that carried fire in their tails…the puppets were just as if they were alive.

Look closely at our philosophers' observed miracles and notice the Nintendo iconography: the raising of flags (levels end in *Super Mario Bros.* with a flag raising up a pole), the holding aloft of parasols (an accoutrement often shown held by the Princess), the impossible carrying of fire (Mario's fireball).

The grisly battleground scene even echoes one oddity found in *Doki Doki Panic*. In a handful of areas you find what can only be described as a decapitated head. The Japanese manual calls him "Big Face." Perhaps a callback to these killed puppet warriors, able to tell their story from the afterlife? Glance again, though, and inspect more closely: Is that head in blackface? The dark skin and wide pale lips would suggest so. Where does this come from? Little explanation is found within the game itself. It acts as a sliding projectile, able to take out enemies as it rolls across the ground. Imagine the shock if, while observing their happy child play their new game on Christmas morning, what looks to be the decapitated head of Al Jolson appears and Mario boots him in the mouth. Thankfully, in the process of tweaking *Panic* for a Western audience, the head was changed to a Red Shell.

Many of the changes made to *Super Mario Bros. 2* during its westbound transformation did more than polish a tent-pole franchise sequel. *Doki Doki Panic* begins with a family jumping into the pages of a magical book. *SMB2* begins with Mario asleep and dreaming, only to wake up and see his dream before him. The choice allows the game to exist concurrently with its immediate prequel, requiring zero connective tissue between the by-then familiar landscape of the

Mushroom Kingdom and this bizarre new world. Yet these catalytic settings have much in common.

Both books and dreams ensnare the participant. Both allow us to be someone we are not. Both are used, either professionally or colloquially, to help identify the owners; Freud wrote a book on dream interpretation for the same reason you scan the bookshelves of a new friend: Each is a window into memories locked away, a catalog of fear and desire. That Nintendo scraped clean the book mythology for their westernized Mario sequel and replaced it with a dream was more of a lateral move than its localizers likely considered. One we choose, and the other chooses us. Books are conscious escapes; dreams allow our brains to roam free, escaping our waking selves.

6.

Super Mario Bros. 2's LANDSCAPE is a tour through our under-accessed realms of imagination. Nintendo's greatest secret is its capacity to tap into this place. Dark creatures live there. Coated in primary colors we accept these strange oddities as children's fare, safe and placid. But Nintendo's past is filled with tawdry reality: rumors of gangster affiliation, the renting of "love hotel" rooms, an ill-advised venture into instant rice. Perhaps Nintendo's present is just one more mask.

Consider some of the terrifying events that occur during a standard playthrough of *Super Mario Bros. 2*:

You throw a mute limbless creature into a pit of quicksand and watch as it slowly sinks.

You jump atop fish, leaping from some unseen valley, in front of a massive waterfall, using their heads as stepping stones to cross the chasm.

A giant snake erupts from the top of a vase, spraying you with bullets.

At the end of the first level, you confront a bipedal lizard with wide eyes and circular mouth. It shuffles back and forth, spitting unhatched eggs and the occasional fireball. Even its skin, bubble gum pink, seems wrong, an errant drop of candy in a bowl of rotted fruit.

Birdo—for this is his name[9]—is no one-off strangeness a bored artist snuck into code. You will see this creature repeatedly throughout the game. And so he shuffles, unblinking, eggs vomited at you until you fling his impossible children back into that oblong head and knock a crystal ball from his stomach. Pick up the orb and your doorway unlocks: A giant falcon head stretches its beak injuriously wide and you, the hero, step inside.

But perhaps the most hellish facet of *SMB2* is less Cronenbergian nightmare and more a return to the simple magic of puppetry: When inanimate objects suddenly come to life.

The game's many underground lairs are often closed off behind locked doors. In order to move forward, you first need to find the key and return. Often hovering above the key room is a triptych of masks. Grab the key and one of the masks stirs, rattling free from its invisible chains and floating off the screen. The first time this

---

9 The original instruction manual includes this bio: "He thinks he is a girl and he spits eggs from his mouth. He'd rather be called 'birdetta.'" To confuse things further, the manual calls him "Ostro," and the ostrich-like enemy is called "Birdo," (They should have both been named "Typo.") In subsequent games, Nintendo has turned Birdo female or neglected to mention gender at all.

happens you might feel surprise, then relief. "Oh good," you think. "It's gone."

What happens next ranks in the upper echelon of Horrifying Game Moments. The now-sentient mask is not gone for long. Soon the blank-eyed face floats back into view, veering swiftly in your direction. You notice in time and jump. Phanto (as the mask is called in the instruction manual) swoops past and slows down; it's turning around. Now it's headed right for you again.

In a fit of panic you throw the key. Phanto diverts its path, floating off-screen with the nonchalance of a relinquished balloon. "That was easy," you think. And again you are mistaken, for right as you nab the key, your pursuer, its unchanging face the very face of malevolence, returns to destroy you.

And if you are anything like me, you will yell out words unfit for a child's ears, coloring a game meant to be fanciful and light into something very dark indeed.

7.

PLAYING *SUPER MARIO BROS. 2* AGAIN, in the two-bedroom apartment I share with my wife, is to re-learn the productivity of cussing. Playing any game, for that matter, bends my larynx into the saltiest shapes imaginable. With time comes an understanding that the game on your screen is nothing compared to life's true challenges. Still, with each fall down a pit or graze of a fireball-spitting plant, my mild-mannered speech pattern gives way to filth. *Super Mario Bros. 2* is not even known as a difficult game. But to a player of limited and rusty skills, i.e., your author, it pushes back.

•

I can't beat the World 4 boss and it's driving me asylum-crazy.

World 4 is, to my mind, the first of the tricky bits in a game that some will finish under an hour and some will bang their heads against for decades. You walk over platforms painted with a light-blue finish, video game code for "ice." This means upon ceasing to push right on the D-pad you will continue to slide right.

I select Toad, hoping his low center of gravity helps maintain my balance. Even so I'm slipping all over the place. Better yet, the platforms crawl with albino pudding creatures, in fact anthropomorphic snow mounds each named Flurry. When I jump to avoid the white mass, what looks like a bee the size of your head flies in from the right. This is no insect suffering from elephantiasis but Beezo, a Shyguy with wings who also wields a pitchfork. Below is a shimmery blue ocean. To navigate the gauntlet requires a deft mix of evasion, timing, and pattern recognition. My fingers are tensed, gripping the back of the controller. I stab my thumb down onto the proper buttons, feeling out the right ratio of jump/walk/slide to land on subsequent ice slabs before jumping/walking/sliding again.

A dozen times I've attempted to traverse this icy hell and defeat its blank-stared inhabitants. Or maybe it was 50. Or 100. On the 101st playthrough, I finally slide through unscathed only to find a small island. A high cliff looms in front of me, un-scalable. Tufts of grass wave in the breeze. One last icy patch extends over a rocky outcropping, the eastern-most part of the level. There's nowhere else to go. I hop daintily over the ice and fall down onto the landmass jutting out over the water. Exhausted and out of ideas, I pluck this last grass-tuft, because what else can I do? It's there. Might as well toss a turnip into the sea as a symbol of good things gone to waste, like my time over the past hour…

… only there is no turnip under the ground. Instead of pulling up roots, I pull up a fully functioning rocket. The soil is fertile here. Some seed planted long ago has sprouted most curiously, for I am now inside a vibrating spaceship. It blasts off and rises straight up off the screen, hurtling past an out-of-sight platform jutting out from the top of the cliff. The ship explodes and I fall safely onto the platform.

After all this ice, what awaits me? A flaming orb wearing a masquerade mask by the name of Fryguy. As this anthropomorphic ball of fire floats in a perplexing sine wave, he spits out what look like sparks one after the other. These platforms should have melted by now, my left brain screams. My little Toad boots should have sufficient friction against the ground for me to evade these fireballs with aplomb, yet all I do is slide on this miracle ice.

I turn to my tattered instruction manual, grasping for any help I can find. The book is 30 pages long, about three inches by five inches, bigger than a wallet-sized photograph but not big enough to frame and set on the bedside table. The cover, with its leaping Mario and the name of the game spelled out in yellow block capital letters, each with a red shadow like a Superman logo, has detached from the rest of the book, ripped from the single staple pushed through paper long ago. Inside are not the answers I need.

"He spits fireballs when he is mad," the manual says. What have I done to anger him?

On my twelfth try, I strike Mr. Fry with a third thrown block. But our friend doesn't gasp and shudder into ash; no, he explodes into smaller versions of himself. The fiery spores hop along the same frozen ground I slip across. We touch and my diminutive Toad freeze-frames, looking out from the screen at the perpetrator of this murder—me.

•

"Damn!" I can't not yell out when trying and dying over and again. My walls have absorbed enough vocal abuse. It has gone beyond cathartic; the noise has become instinctual, automatic, like pulling my hand from a hot stove.

The fact that Nintendo of America decided this game would stroke the egos of the Western world more soothingly than the original Japanese sequel is telling of two things: that original sequel's utter masochism; and, perhaps harder to swallow, my own decreasing motor skills.

Difficulty is a point of contention with many game players. Many crave it, yet lambaste a game that punishes them unfairly. Nintendo's track record in this area has slowly shifted over the years. With games like *Donkey Kong* and *Mario Bros.* in arcades, each "Game

Over" meant another quarter an obsessive player might spare. With the transition into their at-home consoles, tricks to earn lives became the newest currency, figured out through haphazard experimentation, schoolyard chatter, or sheer luck. Challenge wasn't a brick wall impeding progress, but an obstacle for persistent players to knock down.

Not everyone enjoyed the opportunity. As Nintendo desired a larger and larger audience, their tendencies toward challenge wavered, eventually coming to a compromise with the inclusion of a "SuperGuide" in 2009's *New Super Mario Bros. Wii.* If you died enough times, a special block appeared; hit the block and a video played onscreen, showing you how to pass a particular level.

Some decry the shift as a dumbing-down for a mainstream audience not inoculated with decades of button-pressing muscle memory. Others, myself included, see the move as a graceful inclusion, a kind of soft-shoe tactic that opens the door to everyone, not just the most practiced and engaged players.

Super Mario Bros. 2 offers the inverse of standard difficulty curves. Many early games present a static choice of difficulty: Easy, Normal, or Hard. Nintendo often avoids such distinctions, designing games where extra challenge could be sought by a player through supplementary goals like collectables or hidden exits for those patient enough to snoop. A game set to Hard may pump in more enemies or lessen the impact of your weaponry, for instance, directly changing the rules or contents of the levels themselves. *SMB2* changes the player.

8.

ALMOST ALL *SUPER MARIO BROS.* GAMES enact some form of the Hero's Journey. You and only you can go forth and save your kidnapped Princess. The framework is the basest of narratives, a sheer veil draped over the functional but ugly, blunt-edged face of what a Mario game is: a manmade gauntlet, *American Gladiators* without the drama. You push forward into castle after castle for the sheer exercise of it but somewhere, in the back of your lizard brain, you know you're doing this for a noble cause.

Having been a completely separate game first, *Super Mario Bros. 2* does not come with this embedded goal. Since the story conceit of *Doki Doki Panic* involved a family of four banding together to save helpless children, Nintendo could easily swap in Mario and pals, maintaining the four characters and their unique traits. Briefly, the metamorphoses of heroes:

- Imajin the Son became Mario: Average in all things. The standard bearer.

- Mama became Luigi: Highest jumping ability. Slippery footing. Hang-time made possible by peak-of-jump flutterkicking.
- Papa became Toad: The strongest, or perhaps with the lowest center of gravity. Can pull objects up quickly and run with them unaffected; all others are slower when carrying something.
- And Rina the Girl became the Princess: The weakest and slowest, but can hover for a second and a half when jumping, thus becoming the favorite (or crutch) of many players.

In *Panic,* the story is explained with animated cut-scenes. *SMB2's* introduction is stripped down, rendered as two screens of text. The manual provides remnants of the game's storybook origins. Like many fantasies, this one begins mid-slumber.

"One evening," the story goes, "Mario had a strange dream." He ascends a zig-zagging staircase to a mysterious door. Beyond the door Mario hears voices. "We have been cursed by Wart and we are completely under his evil spell," one voice says. "We have been awaiting your arrival."

To save a people from devious captors: motivation enough, one might think. But it lacks the romanticism (and sexism) of most every other Mario title. Who belongs to these strange voices? They finish their screed: "Remember, Wart hates vegetables. Please help us!" Mario awakens, the dream lingering. He and his friends go on a picnic. They enter a cave nearby and see the same door from the dream. With a turn of the knob, the game begins.

As a story, *SMB2*'s premise hits the same narrative notes as an articulate auto mechanic explaining the source of a squeaky brake pad. This isn't Shakespeare; this isn't even *SpongeBob*. But at least the setup hums with a kind of eerie resonance: dreams becoming reality, disembodied voices calling out in distress. There are echoes of some long-ago fairy tale. We care enough to set off in the first place. But caring isn't the point.

Modern characters in games with an emphasis on story often have dialogue rich with motivation or vague notes awaiting interpretation. Relationships form and break apart. Narrative-heavy games push for a kind of connection with these on-screen avatars as not only movable pieces but relatable beings to be cheered, envied, mourned.

Other games, such as *SMB2*, deploy separate characters not as people in the room but as tools to wield. How do you want to tackle this stage? Once you know the layout of any given level, you can exploit a character's strengths or willingly handicap yourself.

The ability to choose your player at the beginning of the level is about more than offering a personalized play style. The Princess's hover is a beginner's magic totem, correcting for a yet-developed depth perception and understanding of the game world's unique gravity. Toad is seen by many as an experienced player's choice. His jumps are shallow, offering little room for error. He runs the fastest, though, and plucks objects from the ground with haste; such speed allows an expert to lay waste to complicated layouts in minimal time, but forces an amateur into quick decisions often ending in doom.

All my cussing might have been avoided had I played with the average-in-all-ways character, the eponymous brother himself, Mario. Yet my stubborn nature insisted on hurtling Toad through each increasingly deadly landscape. Challenge is not always a tenet of play, and *SMB2* proves to be dynamic enough to offer both hardship and ease, struggle and satisfaction, through a simple choice: pudgy, lithe, dainty, or strong.

•

The final stretch before World 4's Fryguy features a sequence of towers. You climb to the peak of one, only to find a door at the top, at which point you descend, the insides swarming with enemies. Make it safely to the bottom and, lo—another tower.

Most players will rise and descend then rise again, happy to follow the game's logic. But a discerning Luigi player might get to the top and sense something just off screen. They get a running start and leap, feet aflutter, pushing against gravity's downward pull, and if they time it correctly and get up to speed they land atop the next tower over, skipping two entire playfields.

Likewise, in one sequence of World 5's nighttime desert, you climb out from an underground labyrinth to a cave, only to see a vase high above and out of reach. If you hold down and crouch, eventually your character will flash, enabling a super-jump nearly twice as high as normal. But only a flashing Luigi can reach this out-of-the-way vase. And with it, one more warp zone is found.

A savvy player in need of extra lives, however, might choose Toad for his super-strength, knowing he can pull up the most coins in Sub-space, giving them more chances at level's end to strike a cherry jackpot of 1-Ups. But his lower jumps and quick feet might make arriving at the end a more difficult task than if you relied on the Princess and her hover.

For some, that choice is what makes *Super Mario Bros. 2* special. For others, it points to a break from the formula, an obvious birthmark from its non-Mario origins, making some question the game's validity as a "true" Mario title.

Which raises the question: Is *SMB2* a "real" Mario game? Of course it is. Just listen.

9.

FOR THE PAST EIGHT YEARS, my day job has been to teach college writing. I've worked at various schools in New England, leading a variety of courses to a wide population of students. I've taught British Literature, Poetry, Public Speaking, Composition. Last week, for the first time in nearly a decade, the subject turned to Mario.

As I settled in at the front of the room, about to take attendance to a room of sleepy-eyed freshman at 8:00 a.m. on a Tuesday, one chipper lad asked me a question.

"What are Mario's overalls made out of?" he said.

He smiled, then put his hands over his mouth, as if to contain the punchline from escaping. I took the question honestly, pacing from behind my desk to lean on its front lip, the seated stance a half-measure between authority and comfort. His set-up was a conundrum, anyway: Mario's overalls were made out of code, not material. But I played along.

"Good question," I said. "Um… denim?"

He pulled his hands from his face. "Denim-denim-denim," he said, mimicking the rapid trio of double-bass notes from *Super Mario Bros.*'s underground theme.

The class exhaled, some laughing, others barely conscious. I nodded my head in appreciation. "Very good," I said, adding, "but only after he goes down a pipe." It was a risk, letting them know what I knew. The student's face lit up in recognition, and then fell away into post-joke neutrality, some vague mix of fatigue and uncertainty. The classroom sounded like a level yet begun. Silent.

•

Kōji Kondo has composed the soundtrack for many of Nintendo's revered franchises. Kondo's compositions are to Mario games as John Williams's are to Spielberg films. And like Williams's scores, some carry a heavier cultural weight than others. Ask your common filmgoer to hum the theme to *Amistad* and be met with uncertainty. But mention *Jaws*—even a toddler could pound out the threatening baritone on their toy keyboard.

The original *Super Mario Bros.* music holds a similar place in our collective memories, accomplishing much with minimal notes. Watch *Jaws* and from Williams's first *duh-DUH* the viewer feels the dead black eyes of the shark upon them. Play *Super Mario Bros.* and Kondo's first seven notes work in much the same way, identifying, infallibly, the action to come. Knock out the buoyant intro ditty—*da-da, dah, duh-dah DAH… da*—and Mario springs forth, skidding around your mind's eye as if you played yesterday. Kondo's best Mario themes go beyond Hollywood and approach Beethoven's Fifth for instant recognizability. Each is a masterwork of efficiency.

Kondo has spoken about how his "Overworld Theme" for *Super Mario Bros.* includes rhythmic cues to help beginning players avoid that first enemy. As the game begins, a Goomba, that plump waddling mushroom, wanders toward you. Jump on accented notes and you'll allegedly evade the passive fungus. The method evokes a whiff of the old *Dark Side of the Moon* plus *The Wizard of Oz* rumor, where the album and film, when played side-by-side, produce a rich confluence of sound and image. But of course this music was created explicitly for the action on-screen. That the tune stuck in our heads for decades is the result of the game and its character's ubiquity, but also its innate charm. For a generation the tune is an audible tonic, on the level of hearing "The Entertainer" through an ice cream truck's jangly speakers.

Super Mario Bros. 2's soundtrack does not boast the same cultural cache. Kondo's "Overworld Theme," first heard on level 1-1, is just as jaunty and dynamic here; in fact, it feels less constrained, wobbling all over the scale, leaping octaves and embracing arpeggios. *Super Mario Bros.*'s iconic music feels propulsive; *SMB2* feels more circuitous, haphazard. Notes swing too high, then too low. Melodies end in wobbling decrescendo. A dancer keeping pace would appear confused.

When Mario first drops from the sky, the music mirrors the descent, a falling triad from high to low G, a full octave. Once grounded, though, the standard main theme kicks in, the same track heard above ground on every subsequent level. Move through this first stage and the track inevitably loops. But this initial sound of descent—High G to Low G—isn't heard again. That was the sound of you falling.

Besides the main theme, two other tracks kick in regularly—the underground theme and the boss theme. Future games will build on this, offering remixed themes for each subsequent world. (In this author's humble opinion, Super Mario World, the franchise's 16-bit debut, is the high-water mark of the series for variation and quality of soundtrack, though I won't join the rest of its critics in deriding the unpopular "Bah!" riffs from the New Super Mario Bros. reboots, even though they sound like baby animal a cappella.)

The repetition at first seems limiting. Only three main tracks for an entire game? *SMB2* was not far removed from the arcade era, where players were lucky to hear two separate tracks. Technological limitations come into play as well; with the cartridge's scant storage capacity, Kondo had sufficient room to compose only a few specific songs. But the repeating soundtrack works.

It holds us in place. We know where we are not only by observing but by listening to our surroundings.

When I play *Super Mario Bros.* and fall down a pipe into that first blue-hued cave, I inevitably bop my head to that funk bass ditty, the same as the punchline to my student's joke. *Super Mario Bros. 2*'s underground theme has less of a snap to it; the weaving minor chords evoke a swaying snake rising from a basket on the streets of Cairo. Perhaps this is one reason *SMB2* has lingered less in the public consciousness than its forebear: So much of the game feels vaguely threatening. Certain levels provoke claustrophobia as you dig deeper into a sand pit, or terror as you evade that flying mask Phanto, or confusion as you seek out a necessary key hidden in one of many unlabeled jars.

And then there's the end-level boss fight music. Enter the room where Wart's trusted minions lurk and be seized with a stuttering pronouncement of doom. The boss music barely ranges between two notes, inching up and down by half-steps like a timid adventurer peeking around a corner. Destroy Birdo, that egg-spitting horror, and the soundtrack switches from perpetual fear to victorious release. A quick triad of notes, coming from an approximated 8-bit brass section, delivers you to your next quest as if greeted by a king's trumpeter. Defeat the end-world boss, be it Mouser or Fryguy or Clawgrip or Tryclyde, and the fanfare is more jovial—imagine

Looney Tunes music as performed by player piano. In Kondo's Mario compositions we hear agonizing defeat and surging triumph, but also the playfulness of a composer who understands that his life's work is the soundtrack for pretend heroism.

•

During the shift from Japanese TV channel tie-in to Western Mario sequel, almost all of the tracks remained the same. Except one.

In *Panic*, when you dig up a magic lamp and open a door to the parallel silhouette world of Sub-space, the music heard here connotes *Doki Doki*'s Arabian theme, a lilting Eastern riff not dissimilar to countless scores given to *Arabian Nights* adaptations or background music at the local Zanzibar restaurant. Now, when a player finds a magic potion and goes through the door to the shadow world, they hear a familiar sound: a muted version of *Super Mario Bros.*'s "Overworld Theme."

Is this mere fan service? Games have a long history of hiding secrets, or "Easter eggs," to be found by the most perceptive players. The sneaky addition of *Super Mario Bros.* music into *SMB2* feels like a secret hidden in plain sight, the brightest egg lain out in the middle of the darkest carpet.

Or perhaps its inclusion reveals a certain lack of confidence by Nintendo, wondering whether its players would accept their makeshift platformer without a few nods to its forebear in name only. This was the sound of nervous executives taking a chance.

The musical nod to its past success gave series veterans the tiniest plank to stand on. Elsewhere, few familiar faces joined in: no Koopas, no Bowser, not even a Goomba in sight. With its still-challenging gameplay and exotic, Middle-Eastern vibe, even high critical marks and front-page coverage on Nintendo's own magazine might not have been enough to convince the millions of Mario fans that this, too, was worthy.

Pause the game here. Listen to the beats of drums, the "Underground Theme" reduced to percussion and bass. The melody's tenor notes have been stripped away. All that's left is the rhythm. Soon the track will repeat; Kondo's sheet music likely includes the necessary instruction, *da capo*, Italian for "from the beginning."

PART III: DREAM FACTORY

The starfish is not a fish. It has no internal skeleton like that of a fish or other vertebrates. Why then should we be interested in dissecting the starfish? Scientists believe that some member of the starfish family became the ancestor of the backboned animals, the vertebrates, many millions of years ago. It is fascinating to see how different they are from vertebrate animals.

—William Berman

1.

WHAT WE KNOW TODAY as Nintendo Company Limited was founded in 1889, under the name Nintendo Koppai. Their first products were hanafuda cards. The 48-card deck was not illustrated with the numbers and suits familiar to westerners, but instead with symbols based on calendar months. Trees, flowers, and animals represented various degrees of good fortune. To ward off cheaters, gambling parlors would use a fresh unopened deck for each high-stakes game.

In 1907 Nintendo began producing western-style cards. This one decision opened the door to a worldwide market, and the eventual global operation that would become NCL. But nearly a half-century went by before the next somewhat reckless change helped cement Nintendo's more family-friendly philosophy, and with it, their fortunes.

Twenty-one-year-old Hiroshi Yamauchi took over the company from his grandfather in 1949. Two early decisions of Yamauchi's tenure reverberate throughout Nintendo's subsequent history. In 1953, he decided to compete with the new high-quality cards being imported from the West; Nintendo was the first

Japanese company to produce plastic-coated playing cards. The decision presaged a future of projects known for their dependability. Once Nintendo made the jump to consumer electronics, their hardware has been famously sturdy, able to withstand the onslaught of a seven-year-old's tantrums after losing their last life.[10]

The next left turn from the young President proved even more lasting. In 1959, Nintendo licensed the use of Walt Disney's well-known characters to be printed on their cards. What was once a product found mainly in gambling halls now extended to living rooms and family car rides. Nintendo experienced record sales and Yamauchi immediately saw the benefit of selling to a wider audience. Why only sell to the parents when you could also sell to their children?

But cards were not enough. Fearing irrelevancy, Yamauchi's Nintendo tested the waters beyond games; they sold instant rice, ran a taxi service, and even operated a string of love hotels. All failed.

One day in 1969, Yamauchi asked into his office a maintenance worker, who was normally tasked with keeping the hanafuda card assembly lines clean and

---

10 One famous example is on display at the Nintendo World Store in New York City; a Game Boy, found in the rubble of an explosion during the first Gulf War, still works, its plastic casing charred and melted.

operational. The worker's name was Gunpei Yokoi. Yamauchi knew Yokoi tinkered with his engineering expertise in his off-hours, building doodads out of spare parts. The holiday season was approaching. Along with Hiroshi Imanishi, a recent law graduate brought in to help refocus the company, Yokoi was tasked with coming up with something new to sell. Something simple but entertaining. "Something great," Yamauchi told him, with the vague elegance of a beachfront psychic.

Soon after, Yokoi showed his boss a retractable claw, made up of crisscrossing plastic rods. You brought together two handles like an overlarge pair of scissors; the pincers extended and clamped down, grasping objects from far away. As a practical tool, this "Ultra Hand" was inefficient. But it was fun to use. Yamauchi decided to sell it as a toy; kids and adults bought them in droves. Nintendo was now, once again, in the entertainment business.

Yokoi helped develop a slew of products based on pre-existing technologies that allowed Nintendo to establish itself as a leader in family-friendly fun. First came the Ultra Machine, a device that lobbed whiffle balls in order to practice hitting, indoors or out; then came the Ultra Scope, a self-focusing monocular that was sold to capitalize on the decade's spy-craze caused by Ian Fleming's James Bond novels. Experiments in electronics led to the Love Tester, a devious excuse for flirtatious kids to hold hands, and a lesson in circuitry to boot: An small electric signal would pulse from the device through those holding hands. Only by maintaining skin contact would the circuit remain unbroken, providing the somewhat arbitrary result.

Yokoi's next invention, a simple light-gun called Nintendo Beam Guns, shot thin rays of light at solar cell-equipped targets. When they exploded in popularity, Nintendo bought out abandoned bowling alleys and refurbished them as electronic shooting ranges; each lane ended with a wall of simulated clay pigeons to be shot down with long-distance flashlights. The first Laser Clay Range opened in Kyoto to much fanfare in 1973.

One year earlier, a small company named Atari introduced a simple tennis-like video game named *PONG* into Andy Capp's Tavern in Sunnyvale, California. Soon more complicated arcade games arrived on both sides of the Pacific, filling up hallways in all those electronic shooting ranges, one more channel down which to funnel your hard-earned cash. *Space Invaders*, at its height, was purported to cause a nationwide shortage in the 100 Yen coin (the functional equivalent of the U.S. quarter). By 1977, Magnavox licensed their own version of *PONG* to Nintendo, who manufactured and sold the game to Japan as the *Color TV Game 6*: their first video game system. They followed up with their first stabs at arcade games, mainly cheap clones of popular games. It wasn't until *Donkey Kong* in 1981 that Nintendo amassed a hit that landed both in Japan and in America.

And with 1983's Famicom, which would be sold in the West two years later as the Nintendo Entertainment System, Yamauchi's company would complete its reinvention from a 19th century gambling purveyor to a leading innovator in what could become the 21st century's signature medium.

Each of these advances in business strategy relied on the same simple idea: building something new from old parts. Yokoi called it the philosophy of seasoned—or lateral—technology. State-of-the-art didn't necessarily equal innovation and wonder. But find a clever way to combine common ideas and you can surprise and delight an audience—for cheap. *Super Mario Bros. 2* is just another example of this very Nintendo way of doing things. Instead of building an entirely new game for the Western audience, they saw what was available, changed a few ingredients, and turned one meal into two.

But even before the magic of moving images on a screen, it was those characters from the Magic Kingdom that indirectly led to Nintendo's own Mushroom Kingdom. That first run of Disney-branded cards and their huge popularity showed the impact of recognizable characters and their effect on young and old. Nearly 30 later, Nintendo would borrow this tactic—placing a known quantity (Mario and friends) over a pre-existing product (*Doki Doki Panic*)—for *Super Mario Bros. 2.*

In fact, such purposeful borrowing was there from the earliest Nintendo video games, with a clandestine Mario sneaking into a handful of games having nothing to do with invincibility stars or power-ups, laying the groundwork for every Mario spin-off title since and establishing the chubby plumber as a most unexpected mascot for the quickly advancing industry.

2.

SHIGERU MIYAMOTO HAS SAID he wanted to create a single character that would consistently show up in various games, referring to this ideal once as "Mr. Video." Mario became this anonymous figure. He donned construction hats (*Wrecking Crew*), sat atop a judge's highchair (*Tennis*), and blew a referee whistle (*Punch-Out!!*). But he only took top billing in a select few games, those platformers for which his jump-sound and coin-collection will be known until all our stage-timers run down.

Since *Super Mario Bros. 2*, however, dozens of games starring Mario have come out, all having little to do with the world of the plumber and his repetitive questing over oblong hills. A representative sample:

- *Dr. Mario*
- *Mario Teaches Typing*
- *Mario Paint*
- *Mario Kart* series
- *Mario is Missing!*
- *Mario's Time Machine*
- *Mario's Picross*
- *Mario Golf* series
- *Super Mario RPG*
- *Mario Party* series
- *Paper Mario* series
- *Mario Pinball Land*
- *Mario Superstar Baseball*
- *Super Mario Strikers*
- *Mario Hoops 3-on-3*
- *Mario and Sonic at the Olympic Games*

Mario is less a character than he is a brand. Scratch that: He's less a brand than he is an industry unto himself. Today, studies show that Mario is more recognizable than Mickey Mouse. Though they dress alike, sharing a fondness for red overalls and white puffy gloves, Disney's mascot has grown arguably less relevant to its company over time, whereas Nintendo continues to lean on the mustachioed one. A new video game called *Disney Fantasia: Music Evolved*, based on the classic animated tale of Mickey as the Sorcerer's Apprentice, even strips the Mouse from the story entirely.

There's a reason Mario was chosen to replace Imajin, the son character of *Doki Doki Panic*: He is the heir to all future holdings. A parent paves the way for their children. Mario is progenitor and spawn, both.

And just as Imajin was replaced by Mario, Miyamoto's original Mr. Video has slowly crept into the spotlight elsewhere, replacing others. Updated versions of *Game & Watch* titles for Nintendo handheld systems retroactively insert Mario and friends into old games that previously starred a generic LCD stick figure. Mario no longer sits on the sideline as a line judge, as he did in 1985's *Tennis*, but instead swings the racquet himself in a series of *Mario Tennis* games. Such momentum would not have happened without his first major sequel on the NES proving the worth of the character's cherubic face being attached to another's body.

Even Nintendo's oldest amusements now star the white-gloved one. Buy a pack of hanafuda cards from Nintendo's online rewards store and, over 50 years after the company's first stumble into children's entertainment, you'll find Mario.

3.

Super Mario Bros. 2 was a financial success for Nintendo of America. The decision to reskin a Japanese-only licensed game worked so well that Nintendo decided to re-release the game in Japan as *Super Mario USA* in the summer of 1992. An advertisement at the time shows the familiar *Doki Doki Panic* trappings: an Arabian castle floating on clouds, the egg-spitting Birdo, and the scowling Wart. But now Mario is front and center, clutching a turnip and ready to throw down. At the bottom of the leaflet, a cartoon Statue of Liberty with anime eyes explains the situation, the same kind of disclaimer that would come on the package itself.

Critics were less than impressed; *Famitsu* scored *Mario USA* much lower than they did *Doki Doki Panic*, even though they were ostensibly the same game.[11] In the fast-moving games industry, five years is an eon; the Japanese critics cited the "old-fashioned game design" and the fact that "it doesn't feel new or fresh at all" for their low scores.

---

11 *Famitsu* uses a four-player rating system, with each scoring the game out of 10. *Panic* garnered a 6, 7, 9, 9. *Mario USA* scored a 5, 6, 6, and 7.

Maybe it was this criticism that emboldened Nintendo to freshen up their most successful, but now aging, titles in a new way. Five years after the original NES cartridge came *Super Mario All-Stars* on the Super Nintendo, an enhanced trilogy of NES Mario games including the original Japanese sequel. In fact, just as Japanese players were treated to the Western version of *Doki Doki Panic,* Gail Tilden had tried to introduce Westerners to the first *SMB2* long before *All-Stars.*

She spearheaded a program to offer a free NES cartridge featuring the Japan-only sequel to all *Nintendo Power* subscribers. "We weren't doing anything with it! [So] I worked up with my *Nintendo Power* agency a campaign called 'The Lost Levels,'" Tilden said. She knew certain players would love to see this unknown, challenging, nearly unfair take on their beloved Mario. What began as Japan's ostracized sequel was to become a freebie given away to *Power* subscribers. A similar promotion worked the prior year, when Nintendo gave away a million unsold *Dragon Warrior* games to introduce the Japanese role-playing game to an unfamiliar audience.

An NES cartridge of the original *SMB2* was made, but Nintendo of America didn't want to confuse the marketplace. "I was bummed," Tilden said, admitting that, "it was really kind of a selfish desire to … help boost magazine subscriptions." Eventually, the game was retitled "The Lost Levels" and included in the SNES cart, *Super Mario All-Stars* alongside *Super Mario Bros. 1, 2,* and *3*.

This would not be the last time *SMB2* resurfaced. In 2001, Nintendo launched its new portable handheld system, the Game Boy Advance, with a game called *Super Mario Advance*. And—somewhat shockingly—this was *Super Mario Bros. 2*, again, resembling the souped-up SNES version with a few added levels and challenge. Now you could find Yoshi's eggs hidden through the levels, a clever retcon inserting the popular dinosaur pet from 1991's *Super Mario World* into a game originally made in the 80s.

Elsewhere, Nintendo began to prepare an even more ambitious plan for reintroducing old games to new audiences.

•

In the early 2000s, Nintendo made much ado about a business strategy described in the book *Blue Ocean Strategy: How to Create Uncontested Market Space and Make Competition Irrelevant* by W. Chan Kim and Renee Mauborgne. To succeed in a crowded market you can't swim with the rest of the sharks; you need to create something—a product, a service, an entertainment proposition—that no one else is creating, thus making "competition irrelevant." Less blood in the water.

Nintendo took Kim and Mauborgne's "Blue Ocean" idea and swam with it. The games business heading into the 21st century wasn't a patch of ocean soiled by a spurt or two of arterial spray; it was a chum bucket sodden in guts. Companies made games and systems for an increasingly vocal sector of the population, given louder voices with the internet's advancing communication tools. But with three major companies vying for this audience—Sony with their PlayStation brand, Microsoft and its inaugural Xbox, and Nintendo—there were fewer seals to chew, so to speak. Nintendo was especially affected by this glut of product all marketed toward the same rowdy sector: males aged 14-25 who didn't want to play with their younger siblings' toys any longer. After the industry-saving success of the NES, each of Nintendo's subsequent home consoles—Super Nintendo, Nintendo 64, GameCube—sold less than its predecessor.

Enter the Wii. With its remote-shaped motion-sensing controller and emphasis on active, inclusive fun, Nintendo dipped their lures into very under-fished waters: As in, the rest of the 250 million households who hadn't bought a system in decades—or ever. Curious present-day players came onboard, enthused by something different. Grandmas bought one for their grandkids and then hogged the controller themselves. Lapsed fans of NES classics, now in their

30s, had money to spend. And this strange new box from Nintendo offered something no other system had before: the ability to download old games.

Or at least the ability to buy them. For years fans had been downloading and playing old games on their computer using emulators, programs that pretend to be other hardware in order to read game files ripped from the original source material. Though illegal to sell and distribute for profit, one could "back up" property you owned (and get away with playing decades of games for free). I chose to pay the piper, or plumber, himself.[12]

On July 2, 2007, new Wii owners could download, pay for, and play *Super Mario Bros. 2*. The service was coined Virtual Console: An inspired term, breeding our present obsession with the ephemeral with that clunky box nestled beneath the TV. The service continued with Nintendo's next home system, the Wii U, and it is often this version of *Super Mario Bros. 2*, a digital download costing five dollars plus tax, that I have been playing while writing this book.

Even when the features remain the same, though, something is different. When a game is re-released, even beyond surface appearances, the very way in which we

---

12 The issue of piracy and widespread proliferation of free copyrighted content is worth further discussion. I suggest Piracy by Adrian Johns.

engage with it changes. Our hands are now on a different controller. Through this device we experience the world inside the game, whatever its identity. Play *Super Mario Bros. 2* in 1988 and grasp a chunky rectangle, tapping two bright red buttons to run, dig, toss, and jump. Play *Super Mario Bros. 2* in 1993 and now that controller is curved, grey, its four buttons, purple and mauve, placed in the shape of a diamond.

In 2001, you're holding a stand-alone device on the subway or in the bathroom. In 2007, you're holding what looks like a television remote on its side, which then resembles purposefully that original rectangle from so long ago.

The Virtual Console version is exactly the same as the original, with even the hardware limitations programmed in. Graphics flicker. Glitches remain, like the one where you drop a potion on a grass tuft, enter Sub-space, and just as you exit through the door you pluck the grass, raise a turnip above your head, and for some reason it sits atop your head like a fibrous fedora.

All of the game is here in front of me. Even if, at times, there's nothing in front of me at all.

4.

LEVEL 1-2 BEGINS WITH what appears to be a dead end. I choose Mario and step out of a falcon head attached to a brick wall. Is it connected to the one I just walked through? Such architectural mysteries are never revealed. I hop forward onto the first of three green columns. They populate much of the aboveground landscape, their wavy green facade giving an organic appearance to what are essentially disguised platforms. They might as well be riveted steel.

But then the platforms stop.

In front of me is a great blue expanse, broken only by a few white ovals masquerading as clouds. Even Luigi, with his long, leg-fluttering jump, or the Princess with her one-and-a-half-second hover, will not be able to leap the gap. My savior comes in the form of an enemy. A short black bird sits on a magic carpet, floating in the sky. After a few hesitant bobs, the bird dive-bombs me. At first I jump over the horrid thing, whereupon it floats back up, waiting to attack again. Pidgit (as my manual calls it) is yet another sad, disfigured animal in the zoology of Subcon: a flightless bird who can soar through the air only by sitting on a mystical rug.

He descends again and I jump earlier this time, leaping upon Pidgit's head. We're flying together now. I can't yet control our movement, though. He continues his midair dance, ignoring me completely. So I lift him above me and toss him into the chasm. His flying rug is mine now. I steer the magic carpet across the sky while avoiding a wave of flying Shyguys. Finally another green platform appears. My carpet blinks in and out, its magic dissipating, and I jump off the carpet before it disappears. I land on a cross-section of grass and, below that, soil. Tall palm trees and squat vases line my way. I push forward until another cliff impedes my progress. The only way forward is through a locked door. Now all I need is a key.

But my impatience is a looming mask, hovering overhead. I'll come back to this door later. Other warp zones await.

5.

Since Yokoi's early experiments, Nintendo has always toyed with our expectations. The original arcade game *Mario Bros.* was one screen large, but the level was less a square and more a cylinder. The field of play wrapped around—go off to the right and you'll appear on the left of the screen. One reason *Super Mario Bros.* was so impactful at the time of its release was the breaking down of this false connection.

Now you could walk to the right... and the world continued. There was more of this place than you could see at one time. The monitor was no longer a wrought-iron fence; rather, it became a microscope, or binoculars, something to look through to see only part of the whole.

SMB wasn't the first game to accomplish this; Hoei Corporation's *Jump Bug* (1981) was the first platform game in which more of the level unspooled beyond the edges of the screen, while Williams Electronics's *Defender* (1980) was the first to feature scrolling of any kind (though your ship flew through a constant band of space that wrapped around itself). But *SMB* blew the possibilities wide open—not only with its bevy of hidden secrets and doorways, but with the sheer scale of its success.

Nintendo seemed to understand the capacity for games as magic tricks. Beyond the aforementioned warp zones lie a bevy of hidden paths and misdirection. Often the exit will be in front of you, calling for your attention. But a curious player will glean surprising riches. Invisible blocks await calculated (or lucky) head-bopping. Stories of discovered secrets flowed across my schoolyard blacktop, details exaggerated in a preview of teenage rumor-mongering.

Though the Japanese *SMB2* followed the same left-to-right progression as the original, the American *SMB2* levels were more unpredictable. Certain stages follow to the right. Others, most often those condensed into a vertical shaft, share *Mario Bros.*'s cylindrical wrap-around technique. Some sections share the malleable tectonics of Namco's *Dig Dug*; instead of running across the ground, Mario et al. must scratch into the earth and dig a tunnel down to a cavern below. What before would be unalterable ground becomes an exit.

Elsewhere what looks like a bottomless pit becomes an entrance. Next time you play *Super Mario Bros. 2* and approach a huge waterfall, take a leap of faith and see where it takes you.

That *SMB2* offers both fields of play, alongside so many other elements rarely returned to since (multiple characters, grab-and-toss mechanic), makes me suspect that a popular name is a creative hindrance. *Doki Doki Panic* began as a standalone title with no previous expectation. Its designers could do whatever they wanted. This same freedom funneled down into its Westernized version. *Super Mario Bros. 3* would fall back into the standard of the original, moving left to right, as a scroll unspools.

In fact, the joy of controlling characters with differing abilities may well have influenced the power-up suits of the beloved *SMB3*, as the two games were likely developed back-to-back, if not simultaneously. Each was a product of Research & Development Studio 4, the group within Nintendo headed up by Miyamoto after his early arcade successes with *Donkey Kong* and *Mario Bros.* And though two years would pass between the American release of *SMB2* and *SMB3*, the Japanese version of *SMB3* came out two weeks after *SMB2*'s stateside release on October 10, 1988.

Super Mario Bros. 2 is a glimpse at Nintendo's creative madmen in their infancy, experimenting with form and function. As a one-off licensed game based on a television company's mascots, they felt free to express any whim, with little concern to fit into formula. Without Nintendo of America's insistence that the Japanese sequel was a poor draw for Westerners, Mario may have remained confined to one direction.

The success of this anti-formula cemented a life-long pursuit of novelty and change within the larger

Super Mario franchise. Subsequent sequels (the cosplay obsessions of *Super Mario Bros. 3*, the groundbreaking dimensionality of *Super Mario 64*, the bold departure of water-pump-as-central-mechanic in *Super Mario Sunshine*, and the gravity-escaping *Super Mario Galaxy*) may not have been so free to experiment, had the first departure proved a failure.

Despite the broad range of talents, Mario isn't the "everyman" he's alleged to be. He's more of a no-man. An un-man. Mario is no archetype of any existing figure, nor would one aspire to be him. He's a figment, a special case with no preexisting corollary. (I'd say like Santa Claus, but even Mr. Claus has an ancestral tie to a real historical figure.)

Nor is Mario the everyman of games. Such a figure belongs to one of two extremes: The abstract geometry of Circle, Line or Dot, exemplified by arcade protagonists circa 1980 like *Pac-Man*, *Berzerk*, or *Missile Command*; or the muscled superhero of modern times, placeholders for the adolescent mirage of power still perpetuated by character design based on uninformed assumptions of who the average game-player is.[13] Mario is simply as Miyamoto first donned him: Jumpman. Mr. Video.

And *Super Mario Bros. 2* was the first time this Mister teamed up with a Miss.

---

13 According to a 2013 study by the Electronic Software Association, 31% of all game-players are females over 18 years old, with males under 17 making up 19%.

6.

IN 1985, TERRI TOLES was looking for warp zones. Now a professor at Eastern Connecticut State University, she published a study in *The Critical Communications Review* focusing on arcade games and their representation of gender. She found that 8% of the games she examined had any female characters at all, and that only 2% made them playable. The two characters out of one hundred? Ms. Pac-Man and a mother kangaroo. The chosen two were a geometric shape and a cartoon marsupial. Human females were deemed unfit to participate, as doers or questers, by the digital clay-molders of the mid-1980s.

Three years later, little had changed. *Super Mario Bros. 2* wasn't the first mainstream game to star a playable female—that honor goes to *Metroid* (1986), whose lady bounty hunter hid under a space mask until you beat the game—but coming on the heels of the original *Super Mario Bros.*, the sequel's inclusion of the Princess feels significant, and a sign of Nintendo's early understanding that the audience for games extended beyond the staid confines of Teenage Boydom. Even if your brother played, so might your sister or your mom. Anecdotal evidence supports the impact such an option gave to its players.

On a Fourth of July visit to Michigan, my best friend mentioned to his wife that I was writing a book about *Super Mario Bros. 2*. "That was my favorite Mario game!" she said. "I always played as the Princess."

Twenty-five years later, players often have no choice in the sex of their playable character. Even the Princess is more often than not treated as a carrot on a stick.

The needle is moving in the right direction. In 2013, three of the biggest console releases were *Bioshock: Infinite*, *Tomb Raider*, and *The Last of Us*. In two of these games (*B:I* and *TLoU*) a male lead either gains support from or must cooperate with a female character. *Infinite*'s Elizabeth and *Last of Us*'s Ellie are integral to the game—not simple treasures to be won but nuanced, human-ish characters. And *Tomb Raider*'s protagonist is one of gaming's most famous leads, Lara Croft.

But a closer look is less encouraging. Neither Elizabeth nor Ellie are playable.[14] They act as assistants or motivations, not pure protagonists: That's what the male character is for. Meanwhile, Croft's legacy is rooted less in character than in the early popularity of her polygonal breasts first admired in 1996, followed soon after by film adaptations starring Angelina Jolie.

The largest release of the year, whether you're counting production budget, marketing dollars, or gross revenue

---

14 SPOILER: You do control Ellie briefly, but only when the male character becomes incapacitated.

from sales, was Rockstar Games's *Grand Theft Auto V*. You are given the choice of three separate protagonists. Though each is male, there's a faint silver lining in the fact that these are no superhuman role models. One is psychotic. One is pathetic. One is ailing and confused. Dan Houser, co-founder of Rockstar Games, explained in an interview with *The Guardian* that his production team spent over one hundred days on location in Lost Angeles, researching the real-world counterpart for *GTAV*'s fictional Los Santos. "The single longest process is always creating the world," Houser admits. So much time and effort was spent on crafting the richly detailed environments in each of *GTA*'s open-world cities, yet no one thought to offer a single playable woman in the series' ten-year history.

Sadly, the success of *Super Mario Bros. 2* did not auger a future of female leads in first-party Nintendo games; the next release from the company's in-house development teams to feature a female playable character, outside of the *Metroid* series, would be *Super Princess Peach*, a platformer released in 2005 for the Nintendo DS, starring the same Princess who helped Mario and pals defend the inhabitants of Subcon.[15]

---

15 Her special moves comprised four separate, volatile emotions: Joy, Gloom, Calm, and Rage. Each was represented on the handheld's lower touch-screen by a heart, adorned with the appropriate facial expression. Tap the scowling Rage Heart, for instance, and Princess lights on fire, causing enemies to burn up; if she jumps, the earth itself shakes with her anger. The morose Gloom power causes her to cry, which somehow makes her run faster.

The ability to hover was nice but it was no Title IX. How many of the 10+ million who bought *SMB2* were young girls? And how many would have passed it by had they been forced to play sporting a pixelated mustache?

My niece and nephew are seven and nine years old now. What interactive characters will stand in for their generation, and will Mario have a place there? On my desk is a bent piece of paper on which my niece drew a picture for me last summer. The arms are short and chunky. The all-pupil eyes cast a fearful gaze. But the chubby nose, overalls, and a telltale M hat identify the quick sketch.

To my knowledge, she didn't even know I was writing this book. Yet she gave me a drawing of Mario, unrequested. She must've known. My sister, her mother, must have mentioned something. But I prefer the mystery, some programmable code in the air pushing us into place, telling us how to move.

7.

To play *Super Mario Bros. 2* well is to feel directed through a specific sequence, each step feeling choreographed by a dancer or martial artist. The best moments are when you recognize that rhythm and, using moves learned along the way, you strike out on your own.

World 6 is filled with sand and walking cacti. When bullet-spitting Snifits aren't harassing you, the ground itself is. Many times throughout my playthrough, I jump over an enemy cactus named Pokey and land not on stable desert soil but on treacherous quicksand, illustrated by scattered black dots moving slowly down into a beige surface. Leap out of the stuff quickly and you're safe; hesitate, though, and soon the sand covers your head and you die. The implication is clear: Avoid quicksand to live.

One section of Level 6-3 questions the assumption. I climb a ladder up from an underground cavern. To the left is a high rock cliff resting atop a pit of quicksand. To the right lies blue sky and a grass tuft, waving in the wind, practically calling to me. The immediate response is two-fold: (1) Move away from quicksand, for it is bad. (2) Move toward grass, for it is good.

Sometimes when the game seems to want you to zig, you should zag. I step away from the ladder and go left, sinking into the sand. My Toad character's mushroom-topped head is almost below the ground. I start to jump, keeping my face just above the sinking surface. I push against the rock face. By jumping and pushing left, I somehow slide just below what appeared to be an impenetrable wall. The screen follows my movement, now completely submerged by the quicksand. But I don't die. Each jump still registers with the game's *boing* sound effect. I'm slowly moving underneath the rock.

The wall is not as wide as first assumed; there is a fissure in this mountain, with an unseen door atop normal sand. Finally Toad's head emerges from beyond the rock and lifts out of the quicksand. I jump free and, in real life, take an unnecessarily deep breath. I enter the door and exit onto a cloud platform hovering above a pyramid. Had I originally gone right, I would have run and jumped through two extra areas, a challenging sequence of hanging vines and underground caves, and climbed a rope to the base of this very screen. I've bypassed two-thirds of the level.

•

Of course there's no underlying motive, no reason for Mario, or any character, to do what they do. They move because we make them move. Without people, the game remains inert. At the same time we make on-screen graphics move, we are also beholden to the strict parameters of the gameworld. Marshall McLuhan writes, "A game is a machine that can get into action only if the players consent to become puppets for a time." We ourselves are, in a way, programmed.

Games are difficult to describe in words because so much is quantified in numbers: scores, lives, health, mana, hit points, levels. There is a direct causal link between input and output. Press the D-pad right; Mario moves right. Press A and he jumps. Even modern, complicated games are the product of distinct, binary operations. There is subtlety and depth here, of course, but boiled down the game, like any computer program, is a series of on-off switches. Humans only have one of those. And it tends to be permanent.

A young kid's first encounter with this program still sparks with sorcery. Hold the B button; friction and pressure give way to voodoo incantations between unseen sensors, electronics pulsing like a beating heart: Now Mario is *running*.

Take your thumb off that button and Mario stops. You are in control. Most of our lives, we are not.

•

On the day this book was first bought, I lost my grandmother to a bad heart.

How are you? I always asked my grandma this, either over the phone or in the midst of a pre-feast hug, and for the last decade or so of her life she always answered the same way: "Still vertical."

On July 2, 2013, Elizabeth Weiss died at Henry Ford Hospital in Mount Clemens, Michigan, at the age of 96. My mom was there, by her own mother's side as she slipped away. So was my uncle, one part of a barbershop quartet and former tuxedo shop owner, the rosy nosed entertainer who always shook my hand in an aggressive earthquake of fist-pumping. In the hospital room, my uncle's greeting—a sedate, quiet grasp—reflected the scene. I arrived an hour too late to say goodbye.

Back in 1988, he and his wife Joanne hosted the family's annual Christmas party the day I first glimpsed *Super Mario Bros. 2*. A quarter-century later, a crowdfunding campaign for Boss Fight Books ended with hundreds buying this book when it didn't yet exist. The same day we made our promise, Elizabeth gracefully kept her own.

Near the end of our time together, one of her cherished friends, an aide at her assisted living apartment, visited the hospital. The morphine softened my grandmother's breathing but did nothing to cloak her wit. Asked how she was, her answer, finally, at long last: "Horizontal."

•

I'm back home in Michigan, staying at my mom's house while the family prepares to celebrate a life nearly a century long. I am to give the eulogy in a few days. I lie on my bed, scratching notes on a printout of text, crossing out names then circling them again, until there's no room left on the page and I crumple up the paper, throwing it in the wastebasket like some sitcom cliché of a worker drone.

My phone buzzes on the guest room dresser. A text message from my wife back in Boston: "I had a dream that we went to Nintendo World." Five days later, my grandmother's body will be cremated, her ashes stored in a mausoleum next to the father of her children and her second husband.

I fly back east, emotionally drained. Upon my return Mario seems thin, an unworthy focus. I pick up the controller. Minutes later I jump and fall into an unknown gauntlet of spikes four screens deep, landing between the safety of split bridges, plunging to my death. I try again and die again, breathing out hard through my mouth. Our new kitten Sam scampers across the floor in front of me and I set the controller down so as not to chuck it at her soft skull.

Why again am I playing this?

I played a lot of games as a kid, often while other family members played elsewhere. Now I'm an adult, one of those arbitrary titles suspect to legalese and societal whims. Is 32 the new thirteen? Can an American male eulogize his grandmother one weekend, only to throw turnips at Wart, tyrant of Subcon, the next? Of course he can. Does he want to, though? And is my use of the third-person pronoun a tactic of cowardice, of distancing myself from these somewhat silly questions meant to weigh responsibility versus play?

Playing is responsible. Nintendo has made a kingdom out of play's necessity. If we could truly set imagined heroics aside, we would have done so centuries ago. I never did complete *Super Mario Bros. 2* when I was younger.

"Continue?" the screen asks. My room is empty but for our two cats. Sam is pawing at my desk chair, like a game character's idle animation after being ignored for too long. Charlie remains oblivious, resembling in shape and countenance the game's final boss. I consider alternatives.

There is no other answer. I press start and head for the last levels.

PART IV: LOST LEVELS

Something more will arise for later, something better. These things fill from behind, from beneath, like well water.

—Annie Dillard

1.

I'M RUNNING ACROSS CLOUD PLATFORMS. Above, giant birds named Albatoss soar across the sky, dropping from their claws sentient bombs named Bob-Ombs. In Mario games, nothing is anonymous. Everything has a name.

My falling-apart manual labels the list of enemies with cheeky passivity. The chapter "Obstructing your way" begins on page 23 with a picture of each enemy in the game. That flashing ball of electricity zooming around a platform? Say hello to Spark. The sad hopping bird weighed down by his mask? This is Tweeter. One could argue these are simply defined species, like a fish named "salmon." If I were a taxonomist, I'd be forced to cede this point. But this is more than made-up biology.

There's a familiarity to the names, as if hugs and high-fives awaited the next encounter and not a swift death. Along with this twinge of camaraderie comes an obviousness that other fictional creations seek to avoid. The only name for a spiny cactus less on-the-nose than "Pokey" is "Spiny Cactus." Tweeter is the kind of onomatopoeic word a pre-lingual toddler spouts to test their speaking skills, not the genus given to an earthbound bird that doesn't even chirp.

My personal favorite of the bunch is Snifit. He resembles the squat cloak-wearing Shyguy, but instead of a standard white cowl, his face is obscured by what looks like a gas mask. Instead of inhaling, he expectorates. As the manual puts it: "[He] spits the bullets of evil dreams from his mouth."

Many names traffic in puns, as is often the case with Japanese naming conventions. A popular feature of Japanese poetry is *kakekotoba*, or "pivot-word." Donald Keene, in his introductory text *Japanese Literature*, writes:

> The function of the "pivot-word" is to link two different images by shifting in its own meaning...
> [This] shows a characteristic feature of the language, the compression of many images into a small space, usually by means of puns which expand the overtones of words.

These pivot-words are classically placed at the end of one line of verse, finishing the previous thought while leading already into the next. Keene gives what he calls a "crude example": What use are riches when you diamonds, / Rubies and gold are dross. Here, diamonds acts as both "die" and the gem itself; actual Japanese poets employ the technique more subtly. Though names such as Albatoss are simpler forms of wordplay than *kakekotoba*, each exemplifies the cleverness of creation through language.

Nintendo of America's localization efforts circa 1988 fit somewhere in between the subtlety of literature and an amateur's crude approximation. Naming a projectile-flinging snake Cobrat is cringe-worthy yet cute. The prospect of a bomb named Bob injects personality into a destructive device neutered by a half-decade of generic icons on video screens. When my Toad jumps atop one and lingers a second too long, and Mr. Omb flashes and explodes, I don't feel the aimless rage of a bystander but instead the particular wrath of a victim. A bomb didn't just explode near me; Bob blew me up. And himself! With one name, I feel a twinge of guilt.

Poetry succeeds on its ability to wring feeling out of a careful constriction of words. *Super Mario Bros. 2*'s host of characters are not simply turnip fodder but peculiar creatures, wrought with purposeful specificity. But none are there to help you. Each is an enemy in your way.

2.

I'm sitting at a Starbucks on Fifth Avenue, warming my hands on a cold, blustery day in Manhattan. Powered up on caffeine, I step onto the street and head toward Nintendo World, the company's flagship retail store in North America.

Each block feels like a more manageable segment of the whole. A single stage. Halal food stands become street corner landmarks, like the vases in *Super Mario Bros. 2,* repeated with subtle variation. The oncoming pedestrians are a wave of Beezos, coming at me at a steady pace until I reach the tall glass entrance to Nintendo World, tucked behind Rockefeller Center and its perimeter of flags.

The epicenter of all things Nintendo is two floors of games, systems, t-shirts and stuffed dolls. Though dominated by kids aged twelve and younger, I'm not the only 30-something in the crowd not attached to a pleading child's hand. More than 200 million kids (and adults) have held a Nintendo-branded product in their palms. Their stories are bound up in a building over 10,000 square feet: 10 Rockefeller Plaza. I'm here to see what remains of *Super Mario Bros. 2*'s legacy, if any at all, in the 25 long years since the game's release.

Inside, dozens of kids sit on a circular bench playing the latest *Pokémon* game, just released weeks prior to my visit. Game cases cover the walls. Shelves overflow with plush question blocks and, among them, a single warp pipe. Shirts blaze with colorful faces from familiar games. I hear a small voice somewhere to my right: "This is the best room I've ever been in."

Strategy guides line a bookcase. One title is a book of sheet music featuring Mario games. I pick it up and look at the table of contents: *Super Mario Bros., Super Mario Bros.: The Lost Levels, Super Mario Bros. 3…* The book skips right past *SMB2*. I flip through its pages; maybe the table of contents is incomplete, a typo? But no: Every other major Mario game's music is included. Is this evidence to some anti-*Mario 2* bias, an official confirmation of its black sheep status?

But then I spy a stack of t-shirts, their fabric stained a deep blue. "Nintendo WORLD," the front exclaims. Above the chunky font, four cartoon characters pull turnips out of a horizontal ground: Princess, Luigi, Mario, and Toad. A near-exact copy of a graphic taken from *Super Mario Bros. 2*'s instruction manual. Even the price tag confirms it: "SMB2 Group," it says, above a price too high for pre-shrunk cotton and dye. I buy it anyway.

A voice comes on over the store's loudspeaker: Some special guests will be arriving very soon, it says. I look around, my head mirroring the movements of dozens of smaller heads, all of us wondering the same thing, hoping the same adolescent dreams: *They're here.*

Mario and Luigi emerge from a backdoor beyond the cashier. Their Stay-Puft bodies lumber through the crowd with the help of blue-shirted clerks. A child to my right is waving furiously as they approach, yelling, "Hi Mario! Hi Mario!" The mascots' wide-eyed stares peer over the child's head, their giant white gloves waving a blanket hello.

A line forms. I join the throng. One by one, the players enter between the space of these two costumed Bros. and nab a photo. Parents snap a picture of their kid with Mario and Luigi, only to give their camera to the next in line and take their child's place. I hand my phone/camera to an employee and squeeze in between the fake plumbers' soft, plushy shoulders. I wrap my arms around their waists. Each hold up a peace sign, or maybe it was the two-fingered "V for Victory" salute, common in Japan. I slap a high five with Luigi, wondering who's behind that giant foam head. I try not to wonder for long.

Then they're led away, their helpers grabbing each by the hand, making sure they don't run into anything or anyone. I'm reminded of circus animals brought out of their cage for all the public to see, only to be locked back up after performing their tricks.

Later that evening, I catch a bus back up to Boston. Upon my return, I pull out the book I bought earlier at a giant used bookstore in Manhattan: *The Arabian Nights*, the epic yarn told thousands of years ago in ancient Persia, the tale of Scheherazade and her many stories. This edition's copyright date is 1990, published by W. W. Norton & Company and translated by Husain Haddawy. On its cover is a piece of art called "Illustration for the Prologue" by Dia Azzawi. The piece depicts what looks to be a jester or clown, but when I look into those two dark eyes peering back at me from its rounded mask, all I see is Phanto.

3.

I'M IN THE FINAL WORLD. I'm nearing the end. And I'm running out of lives.

World 7-1's gauntlet of pain has whittled me down to one life left. Even though only a single level remains, at this rate I won't last long. My only hope: the slot machine.

As I've explained, each coin gathered in Sub-space during the previous level grants you a spin of the wheel. Three columns rapidly spin a sequence of shapes: Turnip, star, cherry, turnip, star, cherry. Push A to stop each column, one by one, hoping for a line-up of identical items or a first column cherry. The simple set-up appears easy to manipulate. Yet up until this point, I have not mastered the necessary timing.

In fact, there seems to be no trick at all. Sometimes I rapid-fire A-A-A. Other times I'll pull the proverbial lever, wait an extra half-second, then press A-A. I close my eyes and press A in time with a far-off beeping noise—a neighbor's oven timer. I stare hard at the screen and *really* look; there must be some tell, some stutter or clue or secret pixel that, if harnessed, will keep me in cherries all day long. I see nothing. When I press

A with no rhythm and nab a life, I think I've finally tapped into its hidden message only to fail, again and again and again.

While scampering across World 7-1's floating clouds, I managed to pluck eight coins—that Toad is a strong puller. Time to make good. The slot-machine screen comes up. I stare again at that first column of rotating shapes. Turnip, star, turnip, Shyguy, cherry, turnip, Shyguy, turnip, star, turnip…

I press A and stop the tumbling icons on those two red bulbs attached by a stem. 1-Up! I can't hit the next two but no matter. Seven tries left.

That first column feels slower now. I'm seeing the cherry clearer for some reason. After nearly ten hours of play, I've homed in on the sequence's indeterminate pace. All other shapes go grey, blur: All I see is a flash of bright red. I press A—another cherry! Another life.

Somehow I've accrued seven extra lives, missing that first cherry only once. I'm endowed with video vitamin C. I'm stronger now, infused with the false confidence only a game of luck can bestow. The final level awaits.

4.

TRIUMPHS OFTEN STEM FROM CHANCE. Ferran Adria, the great Spanish chef and steward of El Bulli restaurant, is said to have invented tomato foam when one of his food experiments exploded. The resultant pulpy mess had a decadent texture; "foams" would go on to headline the menus of avant-garde (and eventually pretentious) chefs for decades.[16] So, too, would Bob-Ombs and Shyguys be featured widely in Mario titles for years after their accidental inclusion in what was never meant to be a Mario game.

Though they escaped the confines of the original Japan-only game, there's a sense that *Super Mario Bros. 2* characters that pop up elsewhere still exude the stench of an outsider. In *Mario Kart 7* for 3DS, you can race against another player locally who does not own the game; they download a mini-version of the game onto their system over Wi-Fi. The convenience comes with a caveat, however; the only character available to the mooching Player 2 is Shyguy, his face covered in shame.

---

16 This shift in public opinion, from fresh to tired, occurs across mediums. Famitsu's scoring of *Doki Doki Panic* compared to *Super Mario USA* suggests Nintendo and Adria are not dissimilar in how their work is perceived over time.

Birdo, the egg-spitting mini-boss that recurs throughout SMB2, has been featured in a few Mario-branded sports titles. But she also appears in *Captain Rainbow*, a Wii game that, like *Doki Doki Panic*, was never released outside of Japan. It takes place on an island of forgotten video game characters. You, as Cpt. Rainbow himself, must traverse the land and help its inhabitants. You find Birdo trapped in a cage, incarcerated for a crime she says she didn't commit. She resembles a child actor who has aged poorly. Her greeting to you ends in an obscenity-laced tirade. Leave her be and she'll yell to let her out, suggesting that others have ignored her even when she offered, as reward, the prospect of fellatio. Let us step gingerly away.

Even props or inanimate objects that hinged on *Doki Doki Panic*'s Arabian setting have popped up later, re-established as central to some overriding Mario myth. In *Super Mario 64*, a memorable sequence has you riding on the same magical flying carpet you first soared on in *SMB2's* World 1-2. When Nintendo re-released the American version as *Super Mario USA* in Japan, they cemented in place these borrowed elements, as if they'd been there all along. Bob-Ombs were just another foreign loan word absorbed into the Mario lexicon. *Super Mario Bros. 2* was no longer a Western anomaly.

A quarter-century later, the game still does not wield the same influence in our collective consciousness as its famed precursor. Few phones blip with *SMB2*'s memorable score, as thousands do with the original's, a constant presence on the Billboard Ringtone Top 200 (yes, they keep track of these things). BLIK sells life-size wall stickers for Mario's 8-bit original, including the iconic question block I have plastered above the doorframe leading into our kitchen. What little nostalgia-driven merchandise that does exist for the sequel is found by scouring Etsy, an online marketplace for handmade crafts. People still care. But their numbers are few.

In an article for film website Cinema Blend called "Box Office Bob-Omb," the author lists five reasons *Scott Pilgrim vs. The World*, the big-screen adaptation of Bryan Lee O'Malley's graphic novel, failed to find an audience. "If you reference *Super Mario Bros. 2* in a movie," Josh Tyler writes, "there's a pretty good chance they won't know what it is."

Mario will outlast us all. *Mario 2*? The game's impact is less inevitable. Trace amounts still proliferate, though, even if the source material gets twisted in the process.

•

The spotlight shines down on Lilly Bordeaux, dressed not in a sequined gown or sultry dress but blue denim overalls. Harvard Square's Oberon nightclub is packed, hundreds awaiting the next titillating diversion from Rogue Burlesque, a local troupe known as much for their oddball antics and amusing narratives as their saucy dancing. Tonight's show? "Talk Nerdy to Me."

Promotional materials feature a naked female chest, the naughty bits covered over with twin Atari joysticks.

Bordeaux's act begins, and three notes in, over the theater's speakers, I hear it: Kondo's overworld composition for *Super Mario Bros. 2*. Lilly adjusts her red poofy hat, the one with an M over the brim. She jumps on a fake Goomba. The crowd wolf-whistles and cackles. She saunters towards a question mark block hanging from the ceiling by wires. Lilly rears back and punches through the bottom; plastic gold coins spray from the cardboard, dousing the audience in game currency. Some scramble to the floor to grab a shiny souvenir; most can't take their eyes off this Super Mario Sister strutting her stuff.

She approaches another block suspended from above and finds a cardboard fire flower emblem. She slips off her blue overalls to reveal red suspenders over a skintight white shirt. As she dons a white cap and begins tossing orange-painted tennis balls at off-stage enemies, I hoot and holler along with my fellow commoners.

But I'm not thinking about the beautiful woman enacting a famous moment from a cherished game. I'm thinking: *Super Mario Bros. 2* didn't have Goombas! Or question blocks! She's getting it all wrong.

•

Nintendo is not ready to forget its landmark sequel just yet. During the writing of this book, they announced and, months later, released a new title for their Wii U console, *Super Mario 3D World*. The game is a lush tribute to old ideas spun with fresh vigor—a consummate Nintendo move. And though it takes place far outside Subcon within the segmented landscapes of a place called Sprixie Kingdom, *3D World* brings back, for the first time, the choice of the four playable characters from *Super Mario Bros. 2* along with their signature moves.

The green guy jumps extra high. The pink lady floats for a few seconds of hover-time. The mushroom dude runs fastest. No turnips sit planted in the ground awaiting upheaval, nor do we see the freakish parade of masked Shyguys and pitchfork-weilding Beezos; this kingdom is instead inhabited by the traditional Goombas and Koopas as seen in three-dimensional space. But the specific callback is at least a sign that Nintendo is willing to replant the fruits, if not the vegetables, of this particular labor.

Nor has the father of *Super Mario Bros. 2* himself forgotten his first creation. *Donkey Kong Country: Tropical Freeze* will release on Wii U two months later, featuring a familiar technique: plucking objects from the ground. The game's producer? Kensuke Tanabe. That a game released in 2014 features a character first born in 1981 (Donkey Kong), created by Mario's maker (Miyamoto), then given an ability first seen in Tanabe's *Doki Doki Panic* speaks to Nintendo's willingness to borrow from themselves. Three decades on, the well has not yet run dry. That's not quicksand; that's a spring of untapped potential. Or a warp zone to somewhere else entirely.

5.

I ENTER WART'S LAIR. An anxious discordant melody plays, a song not yet heard after ten hours of repeating tracks. The wall is lined with inert Phantos; will they chase me with one false step? But no keys lie here. I've opened the last door. Brass horn instruments extend from the ground in front of him. Wart stands on the right side of the screen, an obese toad with perpetual grimace, his wide eyes clenched shut.

•

Endings matter across all cultural forms, but nowhere do they matter less than in video games. A 2011 survey of avid game-players by Raptr.com, an online games community with over seventeen million members, showed that only ten percent of players completed *Red Dead Redemption*, heralded as Game of the Year by GameSpy, GameSpot, C|Net, and others. Let's all drink that in. Nine out of ten players bought, started playing, then put down what was considered to be one of the finest examples of the form. I count myself among that lot, playing about eight hours before moving along.

Imagine if the ratio held true for other mediums. What if, of the 50 million people who bought Michael Jackson's *Thriller*, 45 million never made it past Track 7, "Human Nature"? We've become a society of song listeners, spending $0.99 for a hot single and ignoring the rest of the album. And yes, we all put our fair share of mediocre books down. In some cases the two-minute movie trailer far outclasses its ninety-minute big brother. But nowhere in culture does the final push remain so inconsequential to the overall experience than in games.

And nowhere do endings matter less in video games than in a *Super Mario Bros.* game.

•

As Wart shifts back and forth, he vomits a stream of poison bubbles from his gaping mouth. I evade the first attack. The far horn spits out a turnip, a weapon to throw, but it falls through the floor. A bubble smacks me in the face and I'm down to one bar of health. I catch a pumpkin and toss it at the blubbery fiend; his mouth opens, stunned, his body blinking a hypnotic strobe. But soon he's slinging projectiles at me and I perish. Six lives left.

•

The original *Super Mario Bros.* is segmented into eight worlds, each ending with a castle protected by the nefarious Bowser, King of the Koopas, the same barnacled ragamuffin who stole your sweetheart. And each time you knock the chap into that moat of lava he carelessly stands over, you're met not by your distressed damsel but her fair servant, the Mushroom Retainer (who will become known as Toad), who famously says,

> THANK YOU MARIO!
> BUT OUR PRINCESS IS IN
> ANOTHER CASTLE!

That this happens seven times in a row should teach you, game-player of 1985, that this franchise does not hold climactic narrative moments in high regard. When you finally reach the eighth castle, drop Bowser in the lava, and save the princess, she stands there, unmoving, and bestows upon her savior your hard-earned reward. "Your quest is over," she says. "We present you a new quest." And you get to start all over again.

Future installments only slightly evolve this formula. Later games complicate the battle, where Bowser commands a domed ship, or swipes with his spiky tail, or belches out streams of fire or grows gigantic, the better to stomp you as you've stomped so many of his minions. But each ending is a reiteration of that first final remark.

Nintendo has long tried to stretch the value of a single journey. The only way to truly win *Doki Doki*

Panic is to play and beat the game four separate times, one with each character. The original *Super Mario Bros. 2* released in Japan asked even more of the player. Defeat the first eight worlds and be asked to win again. Only by winning the game *eight* times will the final four worlds unlock. The fact that these worlds are labeled not with numbers but with letters—World A, B, C, and D—is a testament to the effort put forth by those who see them. Numerals are for beginners, the game seems to say. Reach World A and the game truly begins.

But the *Super Mario Bros. 2* that released in the West had no such alphanumeric hidden quest. You didn't need to win using each character; instead, the last screen showed you how many times each character was used during the entire playthrough. The choice feels like another concession to an audience demanding closure. You played and you won. Once.

The final boss of *Super Mario Bros. 2* isn't even Bowser, the now-iconic King Koopa who has plagued Mario in every other mainline title since the first. Survive through all seven worlds and be greeted by Wart. The instruction manual explains, "He created monsters by playing with the dream machine." There's a sense of innocent folly in the description; he was just playing, and all this madness came from a simple mistake.

•

I re-enter this place six more times, all six a failure. I can't master the flow necessary to both evade his attacks and catch/toss the horn-borne produce. What an architectural flaw! To build a lair that creates and transmits that which can kill you…

•

Wart's backstory doesn't resonate with pathos; he's a stand-in for the end, a final steep hill beset with enemy soldiers, something to prevail over. Evil is even too strong a term; the same description calls him "mischievous." This is no climactic moment built on a careful laying-down of foundation. This is a last obstacle, the end point on a line. Mario's hero quest ends as many fictions do: with one last arbitrary test of strength.

•

Down to my final life. A bubble strikes me down, taking one of my final three units of health. I fling a turnip at the toad. I jump, run back, dodge. I stand where I know his attacks won't fall. But then Wart moves forward, changing the eventual landing zone, and I don't predict the shift. I'm hit. I shrink down. One more and I'll perish. An arc of bubbles falls from above. I side-step into a gap and leap for a turnip, catching and tossing the ripe bomb at my attacker. Wart blinks again, stunned for longer this time. He regains his strength.

My hands sweat. My eyes sting. I want this to be over. I avoid, catch and toss again, connecting with lizard flesh. Surely this is it! Wart stops again. He blinks and blinks and blinks. And again begins shuffling to and fro. The masks on the wall behind us do not move, their frozen faces mocking this last drama. The music repeats again, a fifth time, a sixth time. I leap for a pumpkin but it falls too soon. Bubbles miss me by a pixel. I grab a turnip and run in between another spray of poison, then jump to launch my final salvo into his squinting leathery face.

Wart blinks again. His eyes seem to open for the first time. He rises upward in slow-motion before falling, mouth agape, screeching. As he falls, tiny puffs of what look like smoke trail behind him, the final breaths of a cartoon goliath. He's gone. I've won.

After the credits, the final screen depicts a bluish illustration of Mario, nightcap on his head, bed covers pulled up to his chin. Above his head, surrounded in a cartoon bubble, is the last scene from the game. It was all a dream. The whole time, we were never *not* playing as Mario. Written in cursive above the sleeping hero: "The End."

6.

PLAYING A MARIO GAME is about finding secrets. The surface level effort of progressing forward is often enough; you may play not even to "win," but to simply access that sense of control and joy inherent to moving fluidly through his world. *Super Mario Bros. 2*, though distinct from every game in the series, retains that singular feeling.

But participation is not the same as mastery.

•

A Sunday morning in March. I open the *Boston Globe* and see a picture of a young man in his room. "Gamer on quest for Super Mario perfection," the headline touts. The article describes his pursuit of mastering *Super Mario Bros.*, a game that came out years before he was even born, by beating it as fast as humanly possible. He lives down in Quincy, a quarry town south of Boston. He also once held the world-record time for *Super Mario Bros. 2*.

Of the eight million cartridges sold across the globe, one landed an hour south of my apartment, before being cracked open and punished by a now-24-year-old college graduate who works as a cashier at a local supermarket. The name of that store? Roche Bros.

Quincy, Massachusetts is the home of the United States granite industry, settled in 1625 atop catacombs of riches waiting to be mined. The birthplace of John Adams and John Quincy Adams, it's also known as the "City of Presidents." Nearly 100,000 souls live there today. Maybe one day in the near future, the town's Wikipedia entry will include this important detail: home of Andrew Gardikis, Mario Speedrunner.

Speedrunners are the daredevils of video games. Their pursuit—to start and finish a game faster than any who came before—is perversely noble. We question their sanity but can't help being impressed, the way we lionize Chuck Yeager and Sir Malcolm Campbell, those inclined to fly an airplane faster than sound or drive a jet-propelled rocket across the dusty plains of Death Valley, risking death for a few seconds.

To a young man living at home and working at a grocery store, playing a classic video game insanely well was just a way to have fun and be part of a community. So when a representative from Golin-Harris, Nintendo's PR firm in America, contacted Gardikis one day in 2010, he didn't think the message was legit. Someone from Nintendo was emailing him? The 25th anniversary of *Super Mario Bros.* was approaching. They requested his presence for a specific reason: To attempt to break his own speedrun record and be the first person in the world to complete the game in under five minutes. He could not say no.

The event took place on November 7, 2010, at the Nintendo World Store in New York City. Gardikis drove down from his home in Quincy. They treated him like a VIP, letting him in early as a huge line formed along the stretch of storefronts on 48th Street. Eventually Reggie Fils-Aime, president of Nintendo of America, welcomed the crowd and introduced the sprightly Miyamoto, who sliced into a tall, multi-decker cake frosted with the familiar brick and grass levels of his most famous game. Soon the other special guest, less known to the crowd, would be slicing through these same levels.

Gardikis was handed a Wii remote and the Virtual Console version of *SMB* was loaded up. The attendees gathered. Gardikis hit Start. Miyamoto stood right next to him. A few minutes into the attempt, Mario's creator even urged him on. "Break a leg," he told the twenty-year-old.

To try and master *Super Mario Bros.* in front of Shigeru Miyamoto is like performing an experimental surgery on the child of the woman who invented the surgery while she looks over your shoulder. The crowd noise grew. Cameras flashed. Mario scampered across World 8-3. Only one level left. Miyamoto stood there, watching. But then Gardikis fell into a pit. The stage restarted but soon an errant hammer killed him dead. Game Over.

Maybe it was the pressure of performing in front of one of the world's most known and respected game developers. Or maybe it was something else that jinxed his run: As Gardikis leapt across the Mushroom Kingdom, he wore a black shirt bearing the likeness of not only Mario but Luigi, the Princess and Toad, the text "Please Select Player" inscribed above the foursome. He'd referenced the wrong game.

•

It's hazy and wet. I'm walking to a coffee shop where I'll meet the fastest Mario player in the world. To prepare, I watched videos online of Gardikis demolishing *Super Mario Bros. 2.* His approach to Level 1-2, a level that so vexed me with its flying carpet and sky full of Beezos, confirms that he and I are playing the same game but very differently. Whereas I awaited the carpet and its breezy floatation, he takes the aggressive route, leaping with Luigi off the cliff only to land expertly on a far-off Beezo, jumping and bounding from airborne enemy to enemy, before landing safely on the ground below.

When he enters the shop I spy him immediately. The tall, lean frame mimics that of the green-suited other brother, and his t-shirt sports a blown-up image of his weapon of choice: an NES controller.

"I've always been a good runner," he tells me as we take a seat in the back. He ran track in school. He was a sprinter, running in the 100-meter dash, and also did cross-country. But he found it difficult to improve. He could never push his body hard enough. One day, after a few tests at the hospital, his doctor told him he had something wrong with his lungs. He would have to stop running.

In the mid-aughts he watched a speedrun of *Super Mario Bros.* on G4TV, a now-defunct gaming culture channel. He'd been playing old NES and SNES games for years with his older brother and sister. He was impressed by this stranger's play, a single fluid forward momentum with no hesitations. When he played his brother's copy with the intent to beat it as fast as he could, he realized he could perform many of the same moves he saw in the video. He knew he could do better.

Gardikis is 24 now, peach stubble coating a soft face. Ace of Base's "The Sign" plays on the coffee shop's radio. He explains how good it feels to be part of a community where people help each other. He describes his work on tool-assisted speedruns (TAS), where players will use an emulator to go frame by frame through a game and find the exact fastest route; the resultant video is a roadmap to perfection.

While making a TAS you manipulate the game in ways not possible while playing the cartridge at home, to push the program in ways it never expects. While writing the TAS for *Super Mario Bros. 2,* Andrew noticed that, for some reason, if you stand on two flying carpets at the same time, you fly across the screen faster than normal. Figure out how to do that while playing, and boom—precious seconds ticked off.

I ask if I can watch him play *Super Mario Bros. 2.* Gardikis demurs. Unfortunately the game is with his sister, tucked away in a closet. For a world-renowned speedrunner with a *SMB2* clock on his wall, the admission sounds suspicious. So instead I bring the Mario to him.

"I have my 3DS," I say, pulling out the red handheld from my bag. On it are downloaded versions of the original *Super Mario Bros.* and the Japanese sequel. I don't have *Super Mario Bros. 2* yet, but we decide to tap into the coffee shop's Wi-Fi and buy it for $5. I hand the system to Gardikis and head to the counter to ask about the password. When I return I see my 3DS open on the table. On its screen, paused and frozen, is an impossible moment: Mario trapped inside a mound of bricks.

He's in an underground cavern from the first game, a bonus coin room entered through a green pipe. But something is wrong. The Mario sprite is enveloped by the bricks; he's not standing on top of them, or hidden behind, but flush with the brick surface, as if he was ironed flat and stuck to a wall. Normal mechanics do not allow this to occur; the scene is the result of a glitch in the code, and the execution from someone who knows exactly what to do. Gardikis is grinning, pleased with his shenanigans. I push the Start button to unpause the game and Mario slides out from his brick prison.

For a long time nobody thought *Super Mario Bros.* could be beaten under five minutes. In October of 2004, Trevor Seguin held the world record of 5:07. One month later, Seguin bested his own time by one second. Two years later, Scott Kessler reached 5:05. In 2007, Gardikis beat *SMB* in five minutes flat, thanks in part to a single discovery.

Speedrunners try to cut away hundreths of seconds from their records. To knock five seconds off with one move was an achievement of Fosburian heights.[17] He'd spend the next few years trying to be the first person ever to "go sub-five." His record of four minutes and 58 seconds, documented on December 15, 2011, still stands as the fastest time ever recorded.[18]

He shows me the trick he used to set the record. In World 4-2, there is an invisible block that, when hit,

---

17 Dick Fosbury won Olympic gold in 1968 with a new technique used in the high jump he perfected during high school, eventually dubbed the Fosbury Flop, and now the standard in elite competition.

18 On June 25, 2014, a speedrunner known as "Blubber" posted a new World Record time, completing *SMB* in 4:57:69, though he did so using an emulator. Gardikis still holds the console record.

produces a vine that travels to a secret part of the level. That path is the fastest, but there's a problem: When the new level appears, you have to watch as the vine grows before Mario travels up it. If only you could get to that room without needing to take the vine...

I watch as he makes the vine appear, moves forward, goes back to the vine and checks if it's in the right place. He then walks to a pipe that normally takes you below the level, only this time, after he sinks down, he appears on the exact screen where the vine would have taken him.

"Whoa," I say, not for the last time. He restarts the level and performs the maneuver as he would in a speedrun. He races across the level, his left thumb stuttering back and forth over the cross-shaped D-pad while a tiny body on-screen bounds over bricks and Koopas. Then he takes the pipe down and emerges, impossibly, in the room where the vine would have taken him. There is no vine. He looks at me, awaiting reaction. I have no idea what just happened.

•

Night approaches. My decaf Americano has grown cold and undrinkable. The coffee shop will close soon. But none of this matters, because I'm watching Gardikis jump past a Shyguy and then, somehow, jump again in mid-air, leaping onto a high platform otherwise inaccessible.

I ask him what he thinks of *Super Mario Bros. 2* compared to the original, the standard-bearer into which he's logged thousands of hours. "That game is a lot more… [*SMB2*] just has a lot of weird things in it." His comment would make a nice one-sentence summary of this book. The man is an engine of efficiency.

Talking to me, smiling and laughing, his eyes squint as if looking at the sun. When playing the game his eyes are fully open, lids pulled back. On certain jumps he jerks the system up an inch or so. When pushing the B button to dig into a desert level's sandpits, he takes his thumb off the system and pummels the button with his index finger. Playing is very much a physical activity for Gardikis. After doing something amazing, he takes his eyes off the screen and looks at me. Not in a cocky, *"Can you believe how good I am?"* way. He just wants to see my face.

Thousands of people watch him play over their computer, either through live-streams or archived videos, but rarely are they in the same room. I express their collective amazement: the raised eyebrow, the pursued "whoa" lips. A few times I drop my lower jaw open and don't make a sound. When he finally leaps across a cavalcade of Albatosses flying across the entirety of World 6-2, Luigi's feet fluttering from beak to beak with pinpoint accuracy, I say 'Whoa!" again and he looks at me, smiles, squints, before re-focusing on the screen, eyes open again.

Gardikis doesn't hold the world record anymore in *SMB2*. In fact he's moved onto the original sequel, the Japanese *Super Mario Bros. 2* known in the West as *The Lost Levels*. But one day he might return to Subcon. "I can definitely beat the world record," he says, held by Christoper 'cak' Knight with a time of eight minutes and 32 seconds. He and Knight are part of Team Ludendi, a group of runners who push each other and compete at charity events. There's no ill will between the two. Any grudges that come from speedrunning seem to exist more between the player and the game itself.

Before we leave, Gardikis plays a bit of the Japanese *SMB2*. Gardikis is underground, Kōji Kondo's familiar bass line bopping along: *denim-denim-denim.* He sees a gap in the ceiling and tries to do a wall-jump off a green pipe, but slides down. There is no wall-jump ability in the game.

"You catch a pixel," he says, half-explaining the technique while in thrall of the action. Hop up above the pipe and you can run across the top of the level, saving time. He jumps up and slides down the pipe surface. He tries again and again, jumping and running back and running forward and jumping again. No dice.

On the eighteenth missed attempt he says, "I can't do it." But he keeps trying.

He pushes the D-pad right and jumps against the wall, then pushes backwards and tries, again, to jump miraculously off of an invisible pixel, only to slide down, again. I'm standing over him, watching him fail. Customers filled with coffee walk by our table to the restroom. He's staring at the screen. He might as well be in that underground cavern looking for the single pixel, the smallest unit of matter in the game, that will propel him forward and faster than before.

"Come on," he says. Back and forth. Up and down. He keeps jumping and sliding, jumping and sliding. "I can see it, too!" he says. "I can see it." All I see is Mario jumping against the smooth surface of a green pipe and falling down. He's jumped 40 times, now 50 times, now 60 times. "That was really close. I'm mad right now." On the 68th missed attempt he finally sets the system down. If he were at home, and not gripping a stranger's property, he'd still be trying.

"This is my problem," he says. "This is why I'm so good. I don't give up."

His story is the story of Nintendo, and Mario. They keep trying. *Super Mario Bros.* (1985) begat the Japanese *Super Mario Bros. 2* (1986), then the American *Super Mario Bros. 2* (1988), itself a cobbled together stopgap until *Super Mario Bros. 3* (1990). But then what of *Super Mario World* (1991)? And after that, *Super Mario 64* (1996)? Each was an attempt to carve something better out of the same material, to improve upon an already impressive feat.

Numbers and geography turn to atmosphere and beyond: *Super Mario Sunshine* (2002) anticipates *Super Mario Galaxy 1* (2007) and *2* (2010). A quadrant of back-to-basics 2D games titled *New Super Mario Bros.* (2006-2012) acknowledges the past to a fault, not advancing the formula so much as honing and improving past glories to an impeccable, but obvious, shine. Before long we place our chubby brown shoes onto terra firma once more with *Super Mario 3D World* (2013), itself a revamped take on *SMB2*'s mechanics. This is Nintendo's problem, and why they're so good. They don't give up.

The rain has stopped. His frozen café latte is down to an inch of brown slurry. It's time for me to leave. For Gardikis, too. He's lived in Quincy his whole life and is looking to move on. Too many days bagging groceries and weighing fruit. He'd love to one day be a high school math teacher. He enjoys helping others and is good with numbers. At 24, he's an old man on the speedrunning scene. He never thought he'd still be doing this, nearly ten years after he started. But he keeps coming back to Super Mario.

"There's always something to find left in the games," Gardikis says. "You're never going to be finished."

NOTES

1-3

Julian Rignall's review of SMB2 appears in *Computer + Video Games* no. 93 (July 1989). The complete issue (alongside other scans of the magazine) is at the Internet Archive: http://bit.ly/2hxGJUy

The review from the October 1988 issue of *Computer Entertainer* was xeroxed and sent to me by Frank Cifaldi, who has since co-founded The Video Game History Foundation (http://gamehistory.org) to collect, save, and share gaming ephemera.

1-4

Listen to more "Gamemaster" Howard Philips on The Nerdist podcast: http://bit.ly/2hxHGMQ

1-5

The original character of Rina (a.k.a. Lina) was conceptualized as a girlfriend to Imajin, as revealed in the official Yume Kōjō publication *Komyunikēshon Kānibaru Yume Kōjō '87 zenkiroku* [コミュニケーションカーニバル夢工場'87全記録] ("Communication Carnival Yume Kojo '87 Complete Record"). This book was unearthed by Gaijillionaire in his July 17, 2016 video "Yume Kojo! Not The Story of Super Mario Bros 2 vs Doki Doki Panic Nintendo NES History Fuji TV 夢工場87" (https://youtu.be/KL9o9zzCUsQ). The video also showcases some Yume Kōjō advertising material featuring Imajin and Rina in a casual romantic embrace and elsewhere holding hands.

2-1

The complete *20/20* news segment "Nuts for Nintendo" is available on YouTube: https://youtu.be/yt4KG9ib8S4

The complete *Nintendo Power* #1, alongside other scans of the magazine, were available at Internet Archive until Nintendo swooped in and spoiled all our fun. See Allegra Frank's August 8, 2016 Polygon article "Nintendo takes down Nintendo Power collection from Internet Archive after noticing it": http://bit.ly/2aWuPQO

2-2

Chris Kohler's *Power-Up*, once hard to find, is now back in print in a new edition from Dover Publications: http://bit.ly/2hxBDaV. While no longer in print, *Game Over* by David Sheff is still widely available on the used market in several editions and featuring various subtitles. And Jeff Ryan's *Super Mario: How Nintendo Conquered America* was first published by Portfolio/Penguin in 2011 and is now available in several editions and languages.

2-9

Nintendo Magic: Winning the Videogame Wars (Vertical, 2010) by Osamu Inoue, a journalist for Japan's Nikkei Business who was given access to Nintendo's top executives during the Wii phenomenon, is a great resource for insight behind the walls of Nintendo Co., Ltd. The original edition was published in Japanese in 2009 as *The Philosophy of Nintendo*.

3-6

Terri Toles's study "Video Games and American Military Ideology" was published in *Popular Culture and Media Events*, volume 3 of *The Critical Communications Review*, edited by Vincent Mosco and Janet Wasko (Ablex, 1985).

Dan Houser's comments on GTA5 appeared in a September 2013 interview with the *Guardian* entitled "Grand Theft Auto V: meet Dan Houser, architect of a gaming phenomenon": http://bit.ly/2gMVh4e

4-1

Donald Keene's *Japanese Literature: an Introduction for Western Readers* was first published in 1953 in the UK. An American edition followed in 1955.

4-6

Andrew Gardikis's speedrun through SMB2 in 9'15" (a former world record) is here on YouTube (https://youtu.be/Wv6_JrWHFV0). An 8'58" speedrun is also available on his YouTube channel (https://youtu.be/zVLFtPC26xk).

ACKNOWLEDGEMENTS

As much as I enjoy playing video games, most days I like writing and reading about them even more. My thanks to all those strange souls who share the affliction, and whose books gave me hope: Steven Poole, J. C. Herz, David Sheff, Tom Bissell, Ian Bogost, Bill Loguidice, Osamu Inoue, David Sudnow, Jeff Ryan, Eugene Provenzo, Harold Goldberg, Brian Oliu, and my fellow Boss Fight Book authors.

Super Mario Bros. 2 would not have made it to World 1-2 without the generosity and expertise of Gail Tilden, Howard Phillips, and Andrew Gardikis.

Thanks are also due to many saviors along the way, including:

Steve Himmer, for saying my name.

The comprehensive chums at *themushroomkingdom. net*, who provided the net.

Chris Kohler, who emailed me back, even after I admitted to hunting for his college thesis.

Frank Cifaldi, who tapped into his archive of game magazines and provided an unexpected tangent on Prince.

The ladies of Rogue Burlesque, for the inspiration.

Editors Laura J. Williams, Polly Bennell, Jeffrey Seglin, Chris Dahlen, and Clayton Purdom, for reining me in and setting me loose.

Jamin Warren and Jordan Mammo, for the spare beds.

Ryan Kuo, for suffering through the early stuff.

Ryan Plummer, Michael P. Williams, and Joseph Michael Owens, for fine-combing through the late stuff.

Ken Baumann and Adam Robinson, who made these pages look good.

Gabe Durham, who fought off my worst tendencies and championed my best. Your height is no accident.

My family, for their endless and unwavering support. May your love be reciprocated a thousand fold.

And a final thank you to Jamie, my Momo: You give me (nothing but) cherries.

SPECIAL THANKS

For making our first season of books possible, Boss Fight Books would like to thank Andrew Thivyanathan, Carolyn Kazemi, Cathy Durham, Ken Durham, Maxwell Neely-Cohen, Jack Brounstein, Andres Chirino, Adam J. Tarantino, Ronald Irwin, Rachel Mei, Raoul Fesquet, Gaelan D'costa, Nicolas-Loic Fortin, Tore Simonsen, Anthony McDonald, Ricky Steelman, Daniel Joseph Lisi, Ann Loyd, Warren G. Hanes, Ethan Storeng, Tristan Powell, and Joe Murray. We'd also like to thank the good people at The Quarters, an arcade and bar in Hadley, MA.

ALSO FROM
BOSS FIGHT BOOKS